Hedging

A Practical Conservation Handbook

First published in Great Britain in 1975 by the British Trust for Conservation Volunteers,
36 St Mary's Street, Wallingford, Oxfordshire OX10 0EU. Tel: 0491 39766

This handbook is one of a series of conservation handbooks. Production costs of this handbook
have been grant aided by the Carnegie United Kingdom Trust.

Compiled by Alan Brooks. Revised by Elizabeth Agate.

Illustrated by Roy Allitt, Andy Follis and Elizabeth Agate.

Cover illustration by Anne Roper.

ISBN 0 946752 02 8

Published October 1975
Reprinted April 1976
First Revision March 1980
Second Revision September 1984
Reprinted 1986 (twice)
Third Revision April 1988
Reprinted October 1991

Printed by The Eastern Press Ltd., Reading, Berkshire, on recycled paper.

Acknowledgements

The British Trust for Conservation Volunteers acknowledges with thanks the help it has received in producing this publication from the following individuals and organizations:

Basil Blackwell, Publisher, for permission to use extracts from N D G James, 'The Arboriculturalist's Companion'

Bert Clark

John H Connabeer

Michael R Coombs

G Crompton

Robin Dale

D J Davies

Faber and Faber Ltd, for permission to use extracts from J L Beddall, 'Hedges for Farm and Garden'

Dick Gaydon

The Hamlyn Publishing Group Ltd, for permission to use extracts from A D C LeSueur, 'Hedges, Shelterbelts and Screens'

Bob Hall

Jim Hall

Tom Harding

Roy Hawkins

Her Majesty's Stationery Office, for permission to use extracts from 'Farm and Estate Hedges'

M D Hooper

Jack Hough

E Alwyn Jones

T Meredith Jones

Russell Lawson

Frank Malin

Roger Mellors

R O Miles

N W Moore

M McArevey

National Proficiency Tests Council

E Pollard

Ann Louise Rule

S F Sanderson of the Institute of Folk Life Studies, University of Leeds

Elfyn Scourfield, Welsh Folk Museum, St Fagans, Cardiff

Arnold Whincup

The other craftsmen and people with an interest in hedging who were consulted

The staff of the Trust and the members of the Conservation Volunteers who have contributed their advice and experience

Contents

Introduction

This is a Handbook of hedgerow management. It is intended to be used by conservation volunteers and all others interested in maintaining valuable natural habitats and our landscape heritage through manual work.

This is a practical field guide. It first introduces basic problems of hedgerow conservation and changing farming needs and the arguments for and against hedges from various viewpoints. It then goes into the details of hedge planting, early care and trimming regimes, and the step by step techniques for cutting and laying hedges and for repairing turf banks. These are skills possessed today by a decreasing number of farm workers. Real craftsmen hedgers, who can teach their trade far better than any book, do still exist. But they have no way of reaching their most receptive audience - volunteer conservers who give their weekends and holidays to the countryside.

This Handbook deals with farm hedges, hedges with a practical purpose, hedges which are first and foremost stock fences or shelter plantings. Ornamental and garden hedges fall outside this category but there are books and articles aplenty on these. Also excluded are shelterbelts, ie tree plantations more than a row or two wide, although very narrow shelterbelts are like very tall hedges and so warrant discussion. Hedgerow trees are dealt with briefly.

Great emphasis is given to hedge laying, since this is the most highly skilled aspect of hedgerow management and the one for which there is the greatest need for instruction. But why should conservation volunteers, or for that matter farmers, bother to cut and lay hedges? Why not just trim them, which can be done mechanically? Or simply leave them to grow up where space permits? Many hedges in fact don't need to be laid. It all depends on their purpose, which in turn rests on larger questions of land management and geography. But where hedges still serve as stock fences, they must be periodically renewed. Otherwise they become gappy at the base and lose their value as barriers.

There are other reasons for laying hedges even where they are not primarily stock fences. The conservation value of hedges is usually enhanced by periodic laying. Before they can be laid they must be left several years to grow up high enough. Even if kept ruthlessly trimmed before, they now become an excellent habitat for birds. Rotational management ensures that there are always some sections of hedge untrimmed, relatively undisturbed, thicket-like and therefore inviting to wildlife.

Hedges of all sorts have a high amenity value. The look of the landscape, so important to our recreational needs, is most satisfying to most people when it changes only slowly. This is a natural feeling which must be allowed to partly balance the economic pressures demanding a landscape radically remodelled for efficient, intensive and large-scale agriculture. The cut and laid hedge is vital to the landscape of some regions, giving regional identity to fields and country lanes, a regional stamp to the horizon.

Cut and laid hedges also have what may be called a social conservation value. The skills needed to nurture and train a stockproof hedge, like so many crafts representative of our rural roots, are in real danger of being lost. These skills and the traditions which they represent demand our respect and interest. We should try to encourage those hedge layers who still practice and to recruit others who will carry the craft into the future.

When are conservation volunteers likely to work on hedges? Most farm hedge management will always be done by the farm worker and rightly so. But increasingly, farmers and conservationists are exploring means of mutual assistance, perhaps aided by grants or subsidies so that farmers can set aside land for wildlife protection and conservation. Under such a programme it would be possible for farm hedging to be done cheaply yet with reasonable skill by local volunteers or groups such as the Conservation Volunteers, the working arm of the British Trust for Conservation Volunteers.

Many old farms and estates are now kept for public benefit by organisations such as the National Trust or as country parks by local authorities. Here it should be possible to deliberately pursue 'archaic' management for improved amenity and education, management which could include traditional hedging. Hedged farmland occurs on some nature reserves too, and even non-agricultural lands are often bordered by boundary hedges. Funds should be available for hedge management, including periodic cutting and laying, to benefit wildlife. Recently the

At Monks Wood National Nature Reserve a mile of experimental hedgerows were planted during the 1970s. These are managed annually, and should provide records of how hedgerows develop.

Finally, volunteers can help maintain hedges bordering footpaths and accessways, which should be managed integrally with the right of way. Before this can be done, of course, the legal

responsibility for management must be established
and the hedge owner consulted. Riverside walks
and canal towpaths often have hedges which should
be kept up to the same standards as the path,
bankside and water. A changing pattern of well-
maintained hedges, variously clipped, laid and
growing up for laying, adds interest to any
countryside expedition.

Throughout the text, when it is desired to stress
a number of separate points they are listed in
a, b, c order. Sequential operations and procedures are given in 1, 2, 3 order. Words used in
a technical sense, eg 'pleacher', 'binder',
'near side' and 'far side', are listed alphabetically
and defined in the Glossary. In several chapters
the Handbook relies on a few authoritative works
on hedgerows and hedge management. References,
incorporated in the text, give the author first,
followed by publishing date and page number in
brackets. Full listings of these and other useful works are given in the Bibliography.

Measurements are generally given first in
imperial units, followed in brackets by the metric
equivalent approximated to the accuracy required.
Occasionally a dimension, and more often a
product specification, is given in one or the other
only, according to current manufacturers'
listings. For example, edged tools are still
produced in imperial sizes and so no metric
equivalents are given.

It is worth remembering that the chain, 22 yards
(20m), is the basic unit of hedgerow length, has
been for many centuries and is likely to be for
many years in the future. This is the unit by
which most hedgers measure their day's work,
although a few use rods, poles or perches, all
of which equal $5\frac{1}{2}$ yards (5m).

Hedgers, particularly in Wales, still identify
hedging styles by old county names and boundaries.
These have been maintained here for this purpose,
although addresses etc are given according to
the reorganised boundaries of 1974.

6

1   The Hedgerow Landscape

Characteristic Regional Hedges

Any part of Britain which possesses hedges can be identified by them. Giveaway clues may be the way in which they are managed, the type of associated bank or ditch, the outstanding shrubs or the way in which the climate has influenced shrub growth.

Throughout most of the country hedges are trimmed between 3' (910mm) and 5' (1520mm) high to one of several basic patterns (see p 63). In earlier days trimming styles indicated clear regional differences but the advent of the mechanical hedge cutter, too often improperly sharpened and inexpertly used, has left many hedges as yard square splintered wrecks. In some areas hedges are still trimmed with care and character, for example in the uplands of north Norfolk with its many carefully maintained rectangular hedges, some of which are unusually tall. Central Montgomeryshire (Powys) has some beautifully rounded farm hedges, trimmed so that the snow will slip off. One can find other examples, but usually they stand out as exceptions to the general scene. Beddall (1950, p 18) presents a familiar picture when he writes that in the northern counties, the north Midlands and the bleaker parts generally, the naturally stunted hedges are kept close cropped 'until they grow clear around the base and then bulge out like a fat woolly sheep on thin legs'. When allowed to grow too tall they are cut back hard, sometimes to ground level, but rarely laid.

Cut and laid hedges characterize most of the Midlands, Wales and parts of the South West. Unless you inspect a cut and laid hedge before the new season's growth has fleshed out the bones you may not notice that, like any object handled by a craftsman, it has a definite and even beautiful form indicating a regional or local style. The Warwickshire hedge, for example, is as different as can be from the Welsh Double Brush, and for good reason. Although each craftsman puts his stamp on his own work, he also conforms to a hedging tradition which evolved with one main purpose, to make the best possible stock barrier given the local type of stock and the nature of the hedge growth.

Hedges can be divided, as they are at national competitions, into 'sheep fences' and 'bullock fences'. It is not easy to design a hedge that is equally proof against both. Sheep scrabble under a hedge or, if of a tough mountain variety, may jump over it. As one farmer said, 'what they can see through they'll go through, even thorn'. Cattle lean over and on the hedge and rub against any stiff projecting branches. Not surprisingly,

weak hedges give way. Both sheep and cattle may eat new shoots, particularly thorn, growing from the stools of a laid hedge. Their depredations seem to depend on their mood and perhaps on the state of the pasture. Some farmers don't worry, but others say that 'sheep have a poison tooth' and that new lambs particularly relish a bit of fresh hawthorn or 'bread and cheese'. Cattle farmers claim that the worst maimers are cattle. All agree that serious grazing can ruin a hedge, sap its vigour and make it very difficult to lay next time. And most will be glad to argue that their local style best solves their own stock problem given the limitations of soil and climate.

Midlands hedges are primarily bullock barriers. Welsh hedges and those laid hedges which occur in the South West are mainly designed to block sheep. Because of this it is easiest to describe hedge laying styles in two separate chapters, recognising that there are border areas which show features of both the Midlands hedge and the Welsh or South Western type.

Hedges were once laid over a wider area than they are today. Country craft books sometimes have photographs dating from the 1920's or 30's showing hedge laying in Cumbria or the Home Counties, for instance, where today this would be highly unusual. But with increased mobility of workers, laid hedges do turn up in unexpected places. Scotland has never been famous for laid hedges, but recently one was seen in Stirlingshire and they surely occur elsewhere on individual holdings. Pollard, Hooper and Moore (1974, p 191) mention the hunting farmer in Kent who had to send one of his workers to Leicestershire to learn the craft for home use, and while talking to a Cornish turf hedger in Camelford we learned of and visited a nicely laid beech hedge nearby which turned out to have been done by an immigrant from the Isle of Wight!

Coppicing may be the oldest form of hedge management, and remains the most widespread after trimming and laying. According to Pollard, Hooper and Moore (1974, p 191), most hedges as well as woodlands in the South East and perhaps also the South West were once managed this way. The hedge, allowed to grow and then cut at the base every twelve to fifteen years, provided the farmer with firewood, hurdles, timber, rafters, thatching spars and so on. This regime was integrated with rotational farming in parts of Essex and Suffolk and probably elsewhere. After the hedges were cut the fields were put to the plough for several years but when the hedges grew up again the land was returned to pasture until the next coppicing. LeSueur (1951, p 91) adds that, even up to the time of his writing, South

Eastern woodlands were occasionally edged with semi-live coppiced hedges created from the woods themselves. Hornbeam was a common species for this:

> ... the poles are allowed to grow up to about 12', and are then slashed and laid towards the next stool. If this is carefully done a fairly serviceable live side on the field edge can be maintained for some years, but growth is almost entirely confined to the outside. As the layers all come from stools set at wide intervals there is usually too much wood and too little twig growth in the fence.

Beddall (1950, p 19) points out that in the eastern treeless fields, hedges were sometimes allowed to grow 12'-15' (3. 6m-4. 6m) in height. They were kept close-trimmed up to 8' or 9' (2. 4m-2. 7m) high and then allowed to overhang, providing shade and shelter for cattle and horses. Like all tall hedges they were hard to keep stockproof - they tended to grow away at the top and thin out at the base. When this happened they had to be laid and left to regrow.

Shelter hedges are important in certain areas, especially where delicate flowers or fruit are grown. A rigid distinction between shelter hedges and shelterbelts cannot always be made, but in general a shelter hedge, no matter how tall, is only one or two rows of trees wide. Thus a hedge seldom exceeds two yards width unless it has been allowed to sprawl. By this standard the 'shaws' or narrow woodland strips which separate many fields in Kent and Sussex are not really hedges, but the East Anglian fens have gained some willow hedges in recent years as a defence against increasing problems of 'fen blow'. The horticultural districts of south Hampshire, west Sussex and the Wirral have their shelter hedges and in various parts of the country orchards are bordered by hedges up to 12' (3. 6m). The arable fields of Kent, Worcestershire and Herefordshire have low hedges, but in sharp contrast are the shelter hedges around the hop gardens in the same regions. Trimming these tall, thin hedges is quite an operation - Beddall (1950, p 20) says that it used to be done from a tall ladder or else from a cart with raised platform, also employed when stringing the hops and pulled by a 'slow, patient horse'.

Particularly interesting shelter hedges are those of the bulb fields of the Isles of Scilly and parts of Cornwall. Here the weather is mild and sunny but winter gales can ruin the early flower crop. Introduced shrubs including Escallonia and the evergreen Pittosporum crassifolium from New Zealand have been planted to form hedges up to

20' (6m) high. For full effect the fields are tiny, only 60' or 80' (18-24m) square, but the space lost to hedges is justified not only by the protection they afford but also because they allow the slight rise in temperature which causes the bulbs to flower earlier than elsewhere.

Vegetation type distinguishes hedges in several areas. Whether the hedge is mixed or mainly thorn depends on its origin and age, discussed later in this chapter, but local planting customs along with climate have sometimes favoured unusual shrubs, such as fuchsia in the Channel Islands and tamarisk on the Lizard peninsula. Breckland has its pine hedges (really shelterbelts), while holly hedges dominate parts of Staffordshire, and beech hedges edge Exmoor. Then there is the famous beech hedge of Meikleour, Perthshire, which is a third of a mile long and 90' high.

There remain the turf and stone 'hedges' of the South West. Rule (1974) says that in mid- and west Cornwall all mounds that are not regular masonry are termed 'hedges'. On the high downs and moors, especially in the far west, dry stone hedges are common. On the moors and country around Camelford the hedges are of earth capped with stone or brushwood. Throughout the rest of mid- and west Cornwall the hedges are earth banks faced with either stone or turf.

It is the stone or turf bank which is most commonly called a hedge in other parts of the South West. But in any case, when Cornishmen or Devonians talk about their hedges they don't mean whatever may be growing on top but the banks or walls themselves. Quite often, in fact, only grass and herbs find a footing. In other cases shrubs self-seed in and sometimes an assortment of species may be deliberately planted along the crown or 'comb'. Usually these plants are left to fend for themselves although the bank is assiduously maintained against the ravages of cattle and lesser pawing or burrowing creatures. In some parts of Devon and Somerset the living hedge is laid, 'steeped' or 'stooped' as they say, rather as it is in parts of Wales.

The County of Cornwall builds its roadside stone hedges to rigid specifications, as shown in the diagram. Farm hedges are frequently higher than this, 6' (1830mm) and possibly much more where they border a track worn below field level. Whatever the size, they illustrate the general principle now followed that the width at the base of the hedge should equal the height. The justification for such a large bank even today is that it makes an admirable stock fence and shelter. Moreover land drainage is improved by the ditch dug alongside the bank during construction.

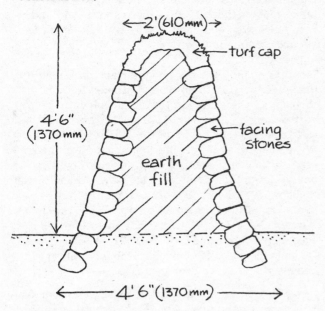

County of Cornwall: Stone Hedge Specifications

Stones to be from 24" × 6" (610mm × 150mm) to 6" × 2" (150 mm × 50 mm) on face; and approx 4" – 10" (100 – 250mm) deep

Irish hedges present another etymological roundabout. They are termed not hedges but 'ditches', as are dry stone walls, temporary peat baulks and other barriers. Throughout the lowland farming country the earth bank is the commonest 'ditch', stone-faced on one side and planted with thorn quicks slipped in among the stones at the base. The ditch-top provides a footing for brambles and gorse (whin), which are used for firewood and shelter. In earlier days the pounded whins were fed to horses. It is interesting that in parts of Wales the bank is likewise known as a 'ditch', although the Welsh dignify the plants growing on top with the name of hedge.

IRISH HEDGED DITCH (section)

Hedges in History

How old is the hedgerow landscape that we see today? Over what time span have present forms of management and regional variations developed? These questions are important not only to the landscape historian but to all those who appreciate the living tradition represented by hedges.

Hedges would have served no purpose until the advent of settled agriculture. Once crops and stock were assigned their respective places on the land, boundaries and barriers became necessary. To try to decide which came first, boundary or barrier, is not quite an exercise in chicken and egg futility, since one tends to imply the other but does not require it. LeSueur (1951, p 11) says that early farm boundaries were often simply marker stones or trees and that hedges were not needed as long as the fields were communal and the livestock herded. In Buckinghamshire, woodland was often marked out by 'bound holes', shallow oblong pits dug at roughly 100 yard (90m) intervals, traces of which can sometimes still be found in Chiltern beechwoods. Alderney's field boundaries were marked by stones until their disruption during German occupation in the Second World War, and similar stones remain today to mark mowing plots in North Meadows in Wiltshire.

Stock barriers have a respectable antiquity too. In fact Caesar stumbled across cut and laid hedges serving just this purpose - though he claims they were to keep out enemy cavalry - when fighting the Nervii across the Channel. Dead hedges, that is interwoven poles or brushy cuttings stuck in the ground, apparently were in use before Domesday as suggested by Anglo-Saxon manorial documents. Dead hedges are known to have been built to fence in deer from the start of the Tudor period (Pollard, Hooper and Moore, 1974, pp 22, 38). The dead hedge was the ancestor of the barbed wire fence, and as such immediately drops out of this history. However it is owed a debt of gratitude as quite possibly allowing many early live hedges to spring up by providing a protected ungrazed strip for colonisation by hedge shrubs. This method of origin is the second of five recognised by Pollard, Hooper and Moore (1974, p 87) as possible for British hedges:

a   Hedges may be around woodland clearings (assarts) made for agricultural purposes. They can either be planted with shrubs taken from the woods or may be relics of woodland plants managed to form hedges.

b   They may be formed by managing scrub growth which has colonised previously unhedged field boundaries or open field strips.

c   They may be planted as mixed hedges of
     which there are many types.

d   They may be planted as single species hedges.

e   They may originate through a combination
     of factors.

Once in existence, hedges were exploited for all
they offered including shelter, firewood and
coppice timber, wild foods such as blackberries
and hazelnuts, and small game especially birds.
By medieval times these products were codified
in law, with 'hedgebote' being the right of
commoners to use the hedgerow for fuel and
branches to feed their stock in winter
(Beddall, 1950, p 37).

These early hedges were probably very rough and
often were allowed to grow quite high before being
cut. Some were wide as well, really linear
thickets more than tidy hedges, and invariably
they grew on banks. Extreme examples, which
can still be found in central Dorset and
occasionally elsewhere, are the double hedges
associated with ancient parish boundaries. When
these are overgrown the central gap is almost
inaccessible, a real tunnel, but if maintained
this gap may have served as a path.

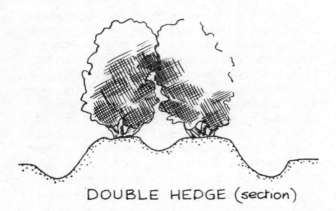

DOUBLE HEDGE (section)

Not all these great double hedges are necessarily
so old; some date from the start of the
Enclosure movement. Witness the case of John
Spencer, who was hauled before the
Commissioners for Inquiry in 1517. He had
bought the manor of Wormleighton, Warwickshire,
in 1506 and had converted the whole place to
pasture. According to Pollard, Hooper and
Moore (1974, p 39), 'Spencer was a grazier and
it is no surprise to find that his fields were
double ditched and double hedged. Part of his
defence at the Inquisition was that hedges
provided fuel for the poor, who hitherto had
burnt straw that should have been used for

cattle. He had set acorns in the hedges because
timber was more valuable than corn or grass'.
Many more depopulated villages in the Midlands
may have been enclosed at this time although few
records have come to light.

Most commonly the big hedges were on a single
bank, and in this form they continued to be built
throughout the enclosed lowlands well into the
19th century. LeSueur (1951, p 12) says that the
tall tree-covered banks of the North and South
West are survivals of this 'bank and ditch' hedge
type, although it seems possible that they may
derive from the early clearance walls in this stony
landscape. Whatever their origin, the later
evolution of the high stone or turf-faced South
Western bank can be traced in some detail.
Pollard, Hooper and Moore (1974, p 98) quote a
Devon account of 1800 which probably referred to
hedges put up in earlier centuries:

> The fences on the first of these improvements,
> were raised upon a base of seven feet wide,
> with a ditch of three feet on each side, and
> which, including the foot for the sods or facing
> to rest upon, occupied about thirteen feet
> width of ground. The mound was raised six
> feet high from its base: the sides faced with
> turf and left nearly five feet wide on the top:
> these were planted with two rows, consisting
> of oak, ash, beech, alder, hazel and hawthorn,
> purchased at 1s 6d per seam or horse-load,
> from those who collected them on the waste
> hedge-rows and woodlands in the country.

Rule (1974) quotes 19th century agricultural manuals
which recommend similar large banks, but made
rather narrower. These apparently were
intermediate forms leading towards today's
precisely-styled pattern, illustrated in the
preceeding section.

The Enclosure movement, which in a sense started
with the Celtic field clearances, really got
underway in the 16th century and from then on
into the mid 19th century proceeded to revolutionise
the open landscape of most of the country. Beddall
(1950, pp 26-7) quotes a sour saying from the
Tudor era: 'Horne (ie sheep farming) and Thorne
shall make England forlorne', but then goes on to
excerpt Thomas Tusser's encomium on hedges
(1573):

> The countrie enclosed I praise,
> The tother delighteth not me,
> For nothing the wealth it doth raise,
> To such as inferiour be.
> There shepherd with whistle and dog
> Be fence to the meadow and corn.
> The horse being tide on a balke
> Is ready with theefe for to walk.

Town layeth for turfe and for sedge,
And hath it with wonderful suit,
When tother in every hedge
Hath plentie of fewell and fruit.
Evils twenty times worser than these,
Enclosure quickly would ease.

This ditty may not have made the poor man's Top Ten but the prospect of regionalising (and appropriating) lands was too tempting for his wealthy neighbour.

Parliamentary Enclosure Acts usually stipulated that newly enclosed lands be marked by boundary ditches and then planted up with hedges on the bank created within. Work had to be finished within a year for the act to be binding, and suppliers of hedging shrubs did an increasingly brisk trade which verged on the frenzied by the middle of the 18th century.

These new hedges were 'quickset', a word which indicates both the hedge itself and the act of planting such a hedge. LeSueur (1951, p 13) says that 'quick' at first meant any living hedge, not necessarily of thorn as later understood. At this time the hedge was still a multipurpose item, coppice for fuel and fencing being as important as thorn for barring stock. He quotes Norden's advice (1607) that the best way to make a 'quick set' is to mix the seeds of oak, thorn and ash together, wind them into a rough straw rope and bury the rope along the top of a bank.

As the rush to plant hedges continued many people found employment gathering wild hawthorn seedlings from the woods. For many years, it was thought that these survived better when transplanted to a bank than would pampered 'nursery' or 'garden quicks'. However, by the 1790's it was realised that proper early care aided the survival and good growth of hedge shrubs. Soon the garden quick was being grown in vast numbers specifically for hedge plantations. It is significant that while wild hawthorn seedlings may have been of either the two British species, Crataegus monogyna, known simply as 'hawthorn' and Crataegus oxyacanthoides, the 'Midland' or 'woodland hawthorn', garden quicks were from the first exclusively C monogyna. It is this species, therefore, which has been the 'typical' shrub of newly planted hedgerows ever since.

Planting 'on the flat', as opposed to setting the hedge on a bank, was rare before the 19th century. It first came into common local use in Yorkshire's Vale of Pickering where as early as 1785 hedges were made by digging a trench, setting the plants along the vertical side and then backfilling.

But it was the advent of the railways which encouraged flat planting, for the engineers preferred their hedges unbanked and often unditched as well. Soon farmers in many areas adopted this practice, which was cheaper and often made for better growth. The old 'bank and ditch' was finally outmoded. Flat planting gradually evolved in its turn so that the most usual modern method is 'ditch and hedge'. In this method a ditch is dug beside the hedge and the hedge is planted on a bank which is so low as to be negligible compared to older banks (LeSueur, 1951, p 13).

A spectacular 19th century type of hedge was the Leicestershire 'bullfinch', a term thought to have derived from 'bull fence'. LeSueur (1951, p 12) quotes an 1832 definition of it as 'a quick set hedge of perhaps fifty years growth, with a ditch on one side or the other, and so high and strong that one cannot clear it'. Understandably, the bullfinch was disliked by fox hunters (and their horses). The bullfinch was cut and laid in the same way as are Leicestershire hedges today, but one wonders if they were left rather higher, since modern laid hedges are ideal for jumping.

The craft of hedge laying probably dates back much further than this, but according to Pollard, Hooper and Moore (1974, p 191) laying was relatively little practised until the 18th and 19th centuries. Beddall (1950, p 31) indicates that at about this time farm leases came to include specific clauses relating to hedge management. In many cases these followed and legitimised local custom. For example, on the Hawstead Estate, Suffolk (1732) the tenant was allowed bushes and stakes for hedge repair. A Warwickshire lease (1786) stated that the tenant was 'when required to cut and plash the hedges and make ditches 3' by 2', or pay or cause to be paid to the landlord one shilling per rood for such as shall not be done after three months notice has been given in writing'. It is not surprising then that hedge laying became a skilled craft and a well-laid hedge a point of pride to farmer and labourer. Indeed some men specialised in hedge cutting, working on a contract basis all winter and hiring out as general farmhands each summer. A few are professionals still, although only one was met during the preparation of this Handbook who now makes a full time seasonal job of hedging.

The Enclosure movement reached its climax in the first half of the 19th century. Thereafter fewer hedges were planted while those that did exist matured and in some cases aged past their prime. In the late 1870's British farming entered a slump from which it has perhaps never fully recovered. Hedgerows on marginal lands suffered both through neglect and through short-term reversals of land use policy. From a wildlife viewpoint, times of neglect may have been the best, especially where hedges were allowed to sprawl into the headlands forming dense thickets. Repeated changeovers from pasture to arable and back again brought the main purpose of hedges into question, for traditionally they had been features of stock-raising areas. But this anticipates today's problems. It is enough to say that despite temporary changes the agricultural landscape looked much the same in 1950 as it had in 1850. It was a landscape formed by enclosure, in which hedgerows and hedgerow trees dominated the scene.

All this time, of course, some parts of the country remained unhedged. The mountains and moorlands of the north and west, much of the chalk belt stretching diagonally from the Yorkshire Wolds to the Dorset coast, a large part of Bedfordshire, the Fens, Romney Marsh - a vast acreage in total. These areas developed their own forms of fencing: dry stone walls, stone-faced banks, wattle hurdles, drainage ditches. Thin lines of trees or shrubs hardly figured here, although the Brecklands and southern Scotland for example had their shelterbelts. So it must always be remembered, when looking at hedges past or present, that whole regions of Britain remain outside the field of view.

Hedgerow Dating

Some hedges are very ancient; many date from the Enclosures; only a few are likely to be less than a century old. Can any more be said? Is it possible to look at an individual hedge and assign its age? Hedgerow dating is a subject of more than academic interest for two reasons:

a Hedges of great antiquity have a historical value which makes them particularly worth protecting. This value can only be recognised if the hedge can be dated by means of historical source material, field evidence or some inherent indicator of age.

b Old hedges tend to have greater wildlife value due to their diversity of component species. The investigation of hedgerow history is directly linked to the survey of particularly 'good' wildlife hedges (see

Appendix A).

HISTORICAL RECORDS AND FIELD EVIDENCE

W G Hoskins has done much work on early field boundaries, tracing written references as far back as the early part of the 6th century in one case. He has outlined the sorts of documentary sources available in 'Hedges and Local History' (1971). County boundaries are among the earliest for which there is precise data, many of them dating from the middle of the 9th century. Anglo-Saxon land charters sometimes go into great topographical detail particularly where borders were disputed. Parish boundaries, which may date anywhere from the 7th or 8th to the 12th centuries, and later divisions within parishes can be sought in old ecclesiastical records. Minor place names can give clues: 'Olditch' on the edge of Dartmoor was known as an 'old ditch' as long ago as 1263. Domesday Book (1086) is reliably detailed for certain parts of the country, allowing identification of important home farm boundaries as they then existed. Ordinary farmsteads are more difficult to trace. By the medieval period park boundaries were becoming important. Cartularies (monastic and estate charters) often indicate new boundaries made to settle disputes.

By now we are starting into the Enclosure Era, with quantities of Parliamentary and legal records worth investigating. Towards the end of this period, in the 1840's, the Tithe Surveys produced some of the finest and in many cases the earliest maps on record for most parishes. They showed every farm, every field and every hedge, and are a basis from which modern changes can be measured.

Changes in field boundaries between those shown on a Tithe Map and those on a post-Second World War aerial photograph or modern Ordnance Survey map can be accurately plotted without physical correlation. But the only way in which the true 'Olditch', for example, can be picked out from all its neighbours is by actually trying to walk it based on the historical topographical description related to such field evidence as now exists.

Pollard, Hooper and Moore (1974) give a number of examples of the uses and possible abuses of field evidence. On occasion it can be extremely suggestive of historically interesting hedged fields which might otherwise go unnoticed. Take the problem of hedgerow length. Scrutiny of the 1:25,000 Ordnance Survey maps ($2\frac{1}{2}$") reveals a remarkable correlation between the lengths of hedged field boundaries and multiples of a chain (22 yards, roughly 20m). The most common length is two hundred and twenty yards, one furlong, ie one 'furrow long'. Twelve and eight chain multiples are next most common, although other lengths may predominate in certain regions. Shropshire, for example, indulges in fifty-five yard (two and a half chain) lengths, with five and ten lengths following on. All indications are that the chain has been the basic unit of hedgerow length for many centuries. In parts of north Norfolk, however, the most common field length is four hundred and ten yards. This stubbornly refuses to fit into any English, Irish or Scottish field unit. The area is rich in Roman and presumed Roman roads, and four hundred and ten yards approximate two Roman stadia (four hundred and five yards). This seems a reasonable match given likely errors in original surveying and modern mapping. The hedges themselves are probably not Roman but the field boundaries may well be.

Field evidence can be misleading, however, unless backed up by other sources. For example, it is known that medieval fields developed a gentle 'reversed S' form because it was the most efficient shape to work using teams of four pairs of oxen pulling heavy fixed mouldboard ploughs. For this reason curved field strips are thought invariably to predate A D 1400, and visible evidence of them today is a sure sign of medieval farming. At Crimscote, Warwickshire, there is a hedge which follows the boundary of one of these field strips, conforming to its reversed S shape. From this one might conclude that it was five hundred years old. But in fact it dates from the post-First World War agricultural depression, when this area which had long been grazed was allowed to grow up in hawthorn scrub. When the land was cleared again for grazing a line of scrub along one furrow was managed to form a new hedge.

Sometimes ancient hedges masquerade as new. Weybridge Forest in Huntingdonshire recently lost almost all its hedges, but until this happened it showed the typical pattern of 19th century enclosed fields. Written records though prove that this system was a realignment of one much older consisting of 17th century assarts from the Royal Forest. Some of the old hedges surviving the Victorian upheaval dated at least to 1652 and probably a great deal earlier since they had once been forest coppice.

INTERNAL EVIDENCE: HOOPER'S HYPOTHESIS

M D Hooper noticed that it was difficult to account for the number of shrub species in a hedge simply through reference to its management, soil type or any other obvious factor. Eventually he decided that the only correlation which did hold true for a wide sample of hedges was one which related the number of shrub species to the age of the hedge. This idea held the key to hedgerow dating by internal evidence. The hypothesis states that, as a rule of thumb:

A hedge will have one shrub species for every one hundred years it has existed, averaged by sampling along standard (30 yard) lengths.

This rough measure is subject to considerable variation, accounted for by climate, soil, differing regional management practices and so on. In a very wide sample this variation or 'error' may be as much as twenty-eight per cent. In a small area some of the regional factors can be eliminated and the variation reduced. The inference is that, given enough local surveys, a whole series of relatively exact formulae could be worked out which would combine to give nationwide coverage.

Why should shrubs colonise a hedge at a relatively set rate? And exactly what is the order of species priority? Experiments are underway at Monks Wood Experimental Station to try to find out and to measure the impact of different management regimes on hedge makeup and ecological balance.

What is understood so far is stated in general terms by Pollard, Hooper and Moore (1974, p 104):

.. the relation between relatively young planted hedges and age is thought to be due largely to simple colonisation by a fairly limited range of species, the relationship of each species with age depending on seed supply, its ability to establish, and its persistence in the hedge. At the other end of the range woodland relic hedges are in one sense of indeterminate age as they will be usually relics of primary clearance of woods in the Neolithic Age. As hedges, they are usually old, much older than most planted enclosure hedges. The dating technique would group them as old hedges but it would clearly not be appropriate to try to give them a particular age using the dating method as their shrub complement will depend in part on what they started with. Very early planted hedges are likely to have several woodland species, as the abundant surrounding woodland would have provided shrubs for planting and a rich seed supply for colonisation. They may be expected

to be richer the older they are in accord-
ance with the dating theory.   More recent
hedges are likely to have been planted
with one species and to be colonised only
with a limited range of species.

One further caution.   The precise figure of one
species per hundred years may not hold true
where there is abundant woodland allowing rapid
colonisation, or where the climate is harsh or
the soil uncongenial and the number of shrubs
species limited, as in the north of England, in
Scotland and in upland areas generally.   Provided
that a local survey begins by correlating species
composition with the ages of known dated hedges,
an accurate local formula should be found.
See Appendix A for a simple survey procedure.

2   Hedges and Conservation

The Loss of Hedgerows

Britain's modern agricultural revolution began about 1950 and has been gathering momentum ever since. Three major trends began to reinforce each other at the start of the postwar period, with disastrous results for the comfortable old Enclosure Era hedgerow landscape.

First, mechanisation finally reached out beyond single or at most linked pairs of farm operations to automate whole sequences of tasks. Machines became far more widely used; they also became larger, costlier and more cumbersome, culminating in the combine harvester which requires a vast capital outlay and can only be run efficiently when manoeuvering time is minimised. Hedges, of course, stand in the way of such machines. In fact, the advent and nationwide distribution of combine harvesters make a good index for the progress of hedge destruction.

Secondly, farm labour continued its long-term decline. Between 1955 and 1965 20% of the work force left for other jobs, and although the rate of loss slowed after this it persisted and seems likely to persist into the foreseeable future. Hedges, particularly laid hedges requiring labour-intensive management, became an unwanted financial burden to many farmers.

Lastly, farming patterns shifted. After the war, dairying and sheepkeeping declined to a record low in the eastern counties while land under tillage became proportionately higher. The reverse occured in the west. Just as important in all regions, many fields which had once been permanent pasture were placed under ley manage-ment, blurring the distinction between grass and arable and requiring machine access to fields which had not previously needed it. Since hedges were now seen to serve little purpose other than stock fencing, more flexible barriers such as barbed wire and the electric fence came to seem more attractive.

Farmers have not been the only ones to remove hedgerows. Urban development of farmland destroyed around 1000 miles (1600km) of hedges each year during the period 1925-1939 and perhaps 700 miles (1100km) a year from 1945 onward. Lesser agents include opencast mines, military airfields, reservoirs and motorways, the latter sometimes creating new hedges along their flanks to make up for some of those destroyed. Pollard, Hooper and Moore (1974, p 68) estimate that in England and Wales between 1945 and 1970 a total of 20,000 miles (32,000km) were lost to various non-agricultural causes as compared with 120,000 miles (192,000km) grubbed up by farmers.

It seems clear that changing farm practices have been the major threat to hedges.

About 500,000 miles (805,000km) of hedges still exist, according to a random survey made by Pollard, Hooper and Moore of aerial photographs dating as far back as 1946. More detailed studies gave an average rate of removal of 0.54 yards per acre (1.2m per hectare) of farmland or a bit over 5,000 miles (8,050km) per year (refers to average annual loss in England and Wales from 1945-70). Figures compiled by the British Trust for Ornithology during the period 1963-6 worked out rather higher but came to agree quite well after correction for the regional bias of the samples. The Ministry of Agriculture 'guess', made by doubling the yearly figure for hedges removed under Ministry grant between 1957 and 1969, of only 1,500 miles (2,400km) lost per year seems unsubstantiated (see Pollard, Hooper and Moore, 1974, pp 59-68). More difficult to assess have been short-term fluctuations in hedge removal, if any. It is nearly impossible to make comparable studies covering different areas in the same year. Pollard, Hooper and Moore think there has been a slowing of the rate to about 2,000 miles (3,200km) per year in England and Wales since 1970, but the Countryside Commission did not confirm this in 'New Agricultural Landscapes' (1974). However, in 'Agricultural Landscapes - A Second Look' (Countryside Commission 1984), it was noted that the rate of removal had slowed in the seven study areas during the last decade, possibly because most farmers had completed their hedge removal by the early 1970s.

The regional pattern of loss is as important as the general rate of removal. What matters in this case is not so much the yardage lost per acre of farmland in each area as the percentage lost compared to what remains. For example, Devon lost 3.5 yards of hedge per acre (8m per hectare) of farmland each year between 1956 and 1961, much more than the national average. But Devon has such small fields and so many hedges that this only meant an increase in average field size from 4 to 6 acres (1.6 to 2.4 hectares) and a decrease in hedges from about 105 to 85 yards per acre (236 to 191m per hectare). By contrast, the same rate of loss in East Anglia would have meant a virtual clean sweep, but here the figure for the same period was much lower. The greatest total loss has been in Huntingdonshire, Cambridgeshire and Lincolnshire, all fairly typical late enclosed areas with large fields and few hedges. The general picture given by Pollard, Hooper and Moore (1974, p 67) is that 'nationally there is a clear distinction between grassland, usually old enclosure areas which are richly hedged and where hedges still have a function, and arable, usually recent enclosure areas where they have little or no function and have gone'. In all areas it is likely that hedges will continue to be lost until the optimum field size is reached for the type of farming practiced.

HEDGEROW TREES

Hedgerow trees even more than hedges are in a perilous position. As far back as 1951 it was found that the replacement of mature trees by new saplings was inadequate. The ratio between size categories for continued replacement should be six saplings per three small, two medium and one large tree (6:3:2:1). Instead it was 2:1:1:1. By 1965 the ratio was even more unbalanced at 1:1:1:1. The long-term future looks poor for hedgerow trees of every species, not just disease-smitten elms. (Suitable hedgerow trees are discussed further on page 56).

The Farmers' Viewpoint

This section lists the comparative advantages and disadvantages of hedgerows and fences and of hedgerow trees, and then evaluates each of the major points of argument.

HEDGES VERSUS FENCES

In order to understand the farmers' viewpoint, and certainly before challenging it, one must realise that hedges have been seen to have bad points ever since the introduction of barbed wire and cheap Scandinavian fence posts a century ago. But traditionally, by comparison with post and wire fences, hedges had more for than against them at least on grazing lands. In recent years the balance has swung the other way, in many minds, particularly where arable fields are concerned. Since upkeep expense is often the strongest argument against hedgerows, it is worth noting that, for the farmer whose hedges need not be stockproof, coppice management may be an easy and cheap way of retaining hedges while keeping them in bounds. Hedges can be cut near ground level every ten to fifteen years, and side trimmed or not in between times as seems best. Coppicing on a rotational basis ensures that some fields are always unshaded and a variety of wildlife habitats remains at all times.

Advantages of hedges

a   They provide shade for stock.

b   They provide a windbreak for crops and shelter for stock.

c   They help prevent soil blow.

d   They provide useful by-products: fruit and berries, faggots and coppice products such as pea sticks, thatching spars, walking sticks, poles for hurdles etc.

e   They provide a valuable habitat for flowers, birds, insects and other wildlife.

f   They provide sport and food: rabbits and hares, partridges, pheasants.

g   They provide visual amenity.

h   They are permanent. With care they can be kept stockproof indefinitely.

i   Maintenance is the only cost once they have been planted.

Disadvantages of hedges

a   They shade crops.

b   They keep the air from circulating among crops at the field edge. This can cause crops to grow poorly and become vulnerable to disease and rot.

c   Their roots extend into the headlands, robbing the soil of nutrients.

d   They take up space which could be put under the plough.

e   They provide a haven for 'vermin', insect pests, weeds and diseases.

f   When they lose their agricultural function and become neglected they lower the visual amenity of the landscape, according to some farmers.

g   They cannot be moved.

h   Maintenance costs are high.

Added to this is another objection which has become very important since the last war:

i   They may block the efficient operation of farm machinery.

Advantages of fences

a   Sun and wind can get at the crops.

b   They take up little space.

c   They can be moved if necessary.

d   They have low maintenance costs.

Disadvantages of fences

a   They provide no shade or shelter.

b   They can injure stock if the animals try to force their way through.

c   They can be broken down by stock or trespassers.

d   They provide no useful by-products.

e   They need to be replaced periodically at a relatively high capital cost. (This may be offset to some extent by farm grants.)

ARGUMENTS FOR AND AGAINST HEDGEROW TREES

Hedgerow trees are a landscape feature in their own right and arguments for and against them are quite distinct from those concerning hedges in general. New planting or selection of self-seeded hedgerow saplings is probably not justified on a straight cost or agricultural basis.

However, where a farmer feels that shade for his stock is valuable, that the timber may be profitable or that the wildlife interest is persuasive, he may manage hedgerow saplings or seek other ways of maintaining trees on his land. Worth considering are plantings which make use of awkward parts of fields that cannot easily be cultivated by machine, such as corners, steep slopes and other 'waste' land. Roadside hedges are good sites, as the timber is easy to extract by machine, and shading of crops is less of a problem.

Advantages of hedgerow trees

a   They provide shade for stock and people.

b   Their timber can be useful and profitable.

c   Trees such as apple, pear, plum and walnut can be planted in hedgerows to provide fruit.

d   They have wildlife value especially for birds.

e   They are a visual amenity, enhancing and diversifying the landscape.

Disadvantages of hedgerow trees

a   Their shade robs crops of light, sun and rain, and can ruin the hedge below them by retarding its growth.

b   The timber may be valueless if it has fence wire, staples or nails in it or is difficult to extract.

c   When cut, the stumps form gaps in the hedge unless left at hedge height. Even then they prevent the hedge shrubs from filling out. Stumps and roots decay slowly, providing a home for fungus and diseases which may infect healthy trees.

d   They harbour bird 'pests': rooks, jays, magpies and pigeons.

e   They can cause the air to stagnate, encouraging diseases. Note that this problem and that of shading can be minimised by limiting trees to two or three per hedge or by increasing field size to 50 acres (20 hectares).

f   Their roots spread into the fields, robbing crops of moisture and nourishment. Elm, poplar and sycamore are the worst offenders. Deep-rooted trees such as oak and lime cause less trouble.

SHADE

A hedge significantly affects the surrounding area with its shade, but only to a distance of one or two times the hedge's height (1h-2h). Crops are affected in the strip next to the hedge, grass less so. Hedges running east-west cast less shade overall than those running north-south, but their north side is shaded most persistently. Individual hedges may be located so that most of their shade falls on 'unused' land such as streams, roads or tracks, in which case the shading argument does not apply.

SHELTER

Claims about the good and bad effects of shelter can only be evaluated once the effects of hedges and hedgerow trees on moving air are understood.

The effects of hedges on wind and other climatic factors

A permeable barrier such as a hedge makes a far better shelter than a solid one such as a wall. The permeable barrier filters and slows the air and cushions that which is forced up over the top. A solid barrier pushes all the air over the top and the air drops quickly on the other side. A solid barrier also produces a low pressure area immediately in its lee which causes the wind to eddy, sometimes at speeds higher than the original wind speed.

PERMEABLE BARRIER (section)

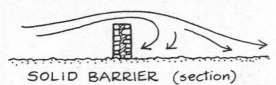

SOLID BARRIER (section)

The optimum permeability is about 40%. The best hedge, by rule of thumb, is one through which movement can be seen but objects not seen distinctly. Clipped hedges may be rather too dense in summer, causing occasional turbulence. Where the sheltered field is in cereals the crop may be 'lodged' along a line parallel to the hedge. In winter most hedges are probably too permeable but the effects of this cannot readily be measured.

The hedge of optimum permeability reduces wind speeds by a signficant amount (more than 20%) for a distance of about eight to twelve times the hedge's height (8h-12h) to leeward of the hedge. For a 6' (1.8m) hedge this is a distance of 48'-72' (15m-22m). Some shelter is afforded up to 30h from the hedge but, while this may affect wildlife such as insects, it is unlikely to make much difference to crops. Some shelter is also afforded the land just to windward of the hedge for a distance of up to 4h, due to a 'pre-cushioning' effect (Pollard, Hooper and Moore, 1974, pp 164-5).

The hedge must be at least twenty times as long as it is high for these shelter effects to work well. Otherwise wind eddies around the hedge's ends and reaches more of the field behind it. Since damaging winds can come from any direction, all four sides of each field must be hedged for full protection. To significantly shelter an entire field with, for example, 6' (1.8m) hedges, the field must be in the order of 48 yards (44m) square (20h leeward shelter effect plus 4h windward shelter effect), or about ½ acre (0.2 hectare). This only makes sense in special situations such as the Isles of Scilly bulb fields.

The siting of hedges affects their shelter value. Long parallel hedges may work well when the wind is blowing at right angles to them but act to funnel and increase the speed of parallel winds. In the

Scillies, temporary shelter screens are placed at right angles to the parallel hedges to prevent this. Gates and gaps in hedges similarly funnel the wind, as can hedgerow trees, which may make certain parts of a field susceptible to lodging.

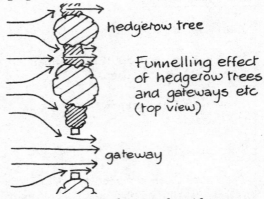

hedgerow tree

Funnelling effect of hedgerow trees and gateways etc (top view)

gateway

A hedge sited along the top of a ridge or on a hillside has its height effect enhanced by the slope of the land behind it, making it a more effective shelter when the wind is in the right quarter. On a flat-topped ridge, however, the cover is only average.

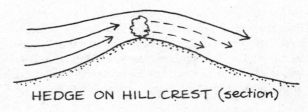

HEDGE ON HILL CREST (section)

Winds tend to be deflected or funnelled into valleys. Therefore hedges most effectively block these winds when located at right angles to the valley.

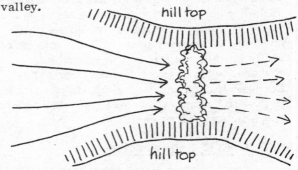

hill top

hill top

VALLEY HEDGE TO BLOCK WIND TUNNEL

The most difficult fields to protect are those which slope into the prevailing wind, which in most cases blows from the southwest. Here the hedge's effective height is greatly reduced and on southerly slopes shading is detrimental to crops.

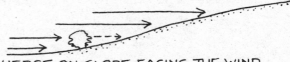

HEDGE ON SLOPE FACING THE WIND

Hedge shelter affects many climatic factors besides wind. Daytime air temperatures are higher and night temperatures lower, but only by one or two degrees centigrade for each. Evaporation is less out of the wind and soil temperature and moisture are higher. The relative humidity is also slightly higher (Pollard, Hooper and Moore, 1974 p 167).

Some people claim that widespread hedge removal goes beyond the immediate influence of individual hedges to alter the regional climate. Experiments on barriers in series do not seem to support this. However a Danish study of two west-east transects running across the country found that average wind speeds were about six miles an hour less along the well-hedged line than they were in the more open landscape. One of the main concerns in Britain is the problem of 'fen blow', where costly seeds and fertiliser can be lost and young crops damaged by the scouring effect of blown topsoil. The danger is considerably reduced where willow shelter hedges are planted and other soil husbandry undertaken. A similar problem occurs on sandy soils, but because these are far less valuable the nation's loss is less even though individual farmers may suffer badly (Pollard, Hooper and Moore, 1974, pp 167-8).

Are hedges needed to shelter crops?

After examining the effects of hedges on shelter, Pollard, Hooper and Moore (1974, p 172) conclude that 'increases in crop yields due to shelter in this country can be expected to be mainly small or non-existent, as water shortage is not common'. An area which could profit by the evaporation-reducing effects of hedges is the Breckland, but here irrigation is probably a cheaper and more effective solution. On the other hand the Scilly bulb fields require high, close-spaced hedges to gain the small temperature rises needed for early flowering, so here, exceptionally, shelter hedges are worthwhile. Shelter hedges may also have value in protecting orchards from frost. Siting and managing orchard hedges is discussed on pages 58-9.

Are hedges needed to shelter livestock?

Many farmers, particularly on exposed hill farms in the north and west, put great faith in hedges to shelter their herds. Stock obviously do seek shelter in heavy rains and gales, although it is interesting to note that they tend to put their backs to the wind and move away from the storm even to the extent of moving farther from shelter. One farmer we met spent many hours training his cows to turn into the wind to reach a sheltering hedge, rather than end up blocked by another

hedge on the exposed crest of a hill. But despite his efforts, shelter's beneficial effects on livestock remain unproven. In fact, recent studies of liveweight gain and food conversion rates indicate no significant difference between sheltered and exposed stock.

Farmers often point to the aid hedges give to the survival of newborn lambs. Other authorities argue that lambs are more likely to be separated from the flock if born at the field edge and that mortality may therefore be greater than among those born with no shelter. Once again experiences seem contradictory and more thorough studies are needed.

INSECT PESTS, WEEDS AND DISEASES

Insect pests

Most insect pests, as well as agricultural weed species, associated with hedges are woodland and woodland edge organisms which have successfully adapted to the cleared agricultural landscape, according to Pollard, Hooper and Moore (1974, p 177).

Insect pests associated with hedgerows at some stage of their life cycle include the leaf curling plum aphid (Brachycaudis helichrysa), a pest of plums and damsons which also lives on blackthorn; the bean aphid (Aphis fabae), the eggs of which overwinter on spindle; the lettuce root aphid which overwinters on Lombardy poplar, a frequently-planted shelterbelt tree; the apple twig cutter (Rhynchites caeruleus), a weevil which overwinters in the rubbish of the hedge bottom; and the small ermine moth (Hyponomeuta padella) which sporadically reaches epidemic proportions but mainly confines its denudations to hawthorn and blackthorn. The looper caterpillar of the winter moth (Operophtera brumata) feeds on the bursting buds, leaves and fruit of a wide variety of timber, orchard and hedgerow trees including hawthorn and myrobalan. Except where the hedgerow provides specific alternate hosts or winter habitats it is difficult to assess its precise effects on pest populations and further studies are needed.

Weeds

The tendency to blame hedges as a source of arable weeds is unfounded. Most of these weeds are annuals which specialise in invading disturbed ground, while the characteristic ground flora of hedges is made up of perennials such as hogweed, nettles and herb bennet which will not invade annually cultivated fields. One plant which does cause problems is couch grass, but the best way to control its spread is to periodically plough or cultivate the headlands and to conduct limited spraying.

The answer certainly is not to spray the hedge bottom with total weedkiller, since this destroys many harmless plants (and associated invertebrates) and may even favour the resilient underground rhizomes of couch, which are left free from competitors (Pollard, Hooper and Moore, 1974, pp 187-8).

Diseases

Diseases such as potato blight and mildews of wheat and oats may occur due to stagnant air near hedges. Hedgerow trees probably cause more problem than hedges themselves if the hedges are trimmed. Trees should be spaced widely.

Hedges are most often implicated in orchard diseases, since blackthorn, crab apple, hawthorn and dog rose are all of the family Rosaceae as are apples, pears, plums and cherries. Certain combinations of orchard and hedgerow or shelterbelt species should be avoided (p 58). By far the most economically serious disease shared by hedges and orchards is fireblight, a bacterial disease of apples and pears. Fireblight reached Kent from North America in 1957; in this country the main outbreaks have been on pears. Laxton's Superb is most susceptible and an initial attempt was made to control the disease by grubbing all trees of this variety, plus any diseased individuals of other types including hawthorns and garden shrubs such as Pyracantha and Cotoneaster. When this failed to stop the disease the campaign was called off, and in fact the effect on hedges in counties such as Kent would have been disastrous if the grubbing had been thorough. The disease spreads via the flowers and by flower-visiting insects, so some help may be had by early trimming of hawthorns around orchards to reduce their flowering. But the disease spores can travel long distances, making trimming no preventative. Apple and pear growers continue to demand allout war on hawthorns while conservationists can only hope that intensive research will find a more acceptable cure (Pollard, Hooper and Moore, 1974, pp 188-9).

LAND TAKING AND MACHINE EFFICIENCY

The issues of land taking and machine efficiency are closely tied. Aside from simple acreage occupied, hedges tend to get in the way of efficient use of land already open. This applies particularly to arable land but increasingly also to pasture which may be periodically sown and mown for hay and silage.

One acre of land is lost to agricultural production in every mile and a half of average hedgerow (1 hectare per 6km). Where hedges are on wide banks, as in Devon, the land lost is one acre in every half mile of hedge (1 hectare per 2km). In all, British hedges take up something like 400,000 acres (Pollard, Hooper and Moore, 1974, p 200). Increasingly, this is land which farmers want to exploit.

By grubbing hedges to enlarge their fields, farmers gain not only more productive acreage, but improved machine efficiency as well. Time wasted in turning at the ends of short rows is reduced. Long straight runs of at least 500 yards (457m) are needed before the biggest machines start to pay their way. Also, small fields waste more seed, spray and fertiliser since inevitably some must go onto the headlands to ensure full coverage of the fields themselves.

As fields size increases, gains achieved by removing more hedgerow become progressively less. In a 100 acre (40 hectare) plot with 5 acre (2 hectare) fields, 2.6 acres (1.1 hectares) are gained by removing all the hedges, assuming they are 6' (1.8m) wide. If the fields are 50 acres (20 hectares) to begin with, 0.8 acres (0.3 hectares) is gained by complete hedge removal. Removing the hedge around a single 100 acre (40 hectare) field gains only 0.6 acres (0.2 hectares), probably not worth the time and expense. In terms of machine efficiency also, the gains of grubbing decrease progressively as the field size increases. On both counts the maximum field size worth creating through hedge clearance appears to be about 50 acres (Pollard, Hooper and Moore, 1974, p 200).

When it comes to decisions on the ground, farmers look at field shape as much as size to evaluate land use efficiency. Fifty acre (20 hectare) fields are optimum for machines only if the fields are roughly square. If the fields are very narrow, space and machine time is wasted whatever the length of the rows. Even those farmers most fond of hedges regret acute angles and inaccessible field corners. Past plantings may have been based on small land transfers or other historical vagaries which are out of keeping with present boundaries. Judicious hedge grubbing can open up cast-off fields and create more regular patterns without destroying the overall 'hedginess' of the farm. Where old gates in hedgerows are too narrow for today's machines, any farmer will grub out a yard or two on each side to be able to use the entrance.

COSTS

The farmer's major argument for grubbing up hedges, or for killing them off as best he can by cutting or burning, is the excessive cost of hedge maintenance. This is usually assumed to far outweigh the cost of erecting and maintaining fences over the same ground. But just what are the comparative costs of hedges and fences?

Any costing must be taken as a rough guide only, since labour and materials increase so fast that estimates are soon outdated. Where fences replace hedges, the cost of grubbing the hedges should be accounted for although generalisation is difficult. Grubbing costs can be very high, around £800 per mile (1.6km) if done by contractor, but are substantially less if the farmer does the job himself with his own machines during slack periods. Large contract machines are often needed however, and each case must be investigated individually.

The cost of a newly planted hawthorn hedge

It is assumed here that, once planted, the hedge is trimmed for seven years and then left to grow for three years before laying. It is then laid at fifteen year intervals and trimmed annually except for the first two years after laying and the three years preceding laying, when it 'lies fallow'. This management regime may be taken as typical, but costs may alter substantially if other programmes are adopted.

Eighty years ago a hedger made three shillings for laying a chain of hedge. Estimates in 1984 are for between £30 and £35 per chain.

The tables below are based on those given by Pollard, Hooper and Moore (1974, p 203), updated to 1984 prices. All prices are approximate only, as they will vary greatly with circumstances.

No allowance is made for inflation, under the assumption that it will affect all costs by roughly the same percentage.

Item	£ per chain (22 yd, 20 m)
Ground preparation, supply and planting of double row quickthorn	70.00
Cattle-proof fence of two lines of barbed wire, posts at 7 yard intervals with intended life 4-5 years	30.00

Mechanical trimming for seven years @ £0.50 per year	3.50
Initial laying (after ten years)	33.00
Trimming for ten years	5.00
Laying (year twenty five)	33.00
Trimming for ten years	5.00
Laying (year forty)	33.00
Trimming for ten years	5.00
Laying (year fifty five)	33.00
Trimming for three years	1.50
Total cost after sixty years	252.00

Pro-rated annual cost about £4.20 per chain.

The cost of an existing mature hawthorn hedge

The same assumptions are made here as in the example above. The only difference is that it is assumed that there is no planting and establishment cost but that the hedge is ready to lay in year one. This is the likely case on most farms, where hedges are already mature but in some need of attention.

Item	£ per chain
Laying (years one, fifteen, thirty, forty five and sixty) @ £33.00	165.00
Trimming for a total of forty years @ £0.50 per year	20.00
Total cost after 60 years	185.00

Pro-rated annual cost about £3.08 per chain.

The cost of a cattle proof fence

This is for a fence of three lines of mild steel barbed wire, with posts at 2 yard intervals. If sheep netting or rabbit netting is required the cost will be higher. It is assumed that the fence must be replaced at twenty year intervals.

Item	£ per chain
Erection (year one)	35.00
Annual maintenance	nil
Replacement (year twenty)	35.00
Replacement (year forty)	35.00
Replacement (year sixty)	35.00
Total cost after sixty years	140.00
Total cost after eighty years (before next replacement)	140.00

The pro-rated annual cost, if taken at the time time of replacement, is about £2.35 per chain. However, if the cost is pro-rated at the end of the fence's life, in year eighty, the annual expense is about £1.75 per chain.

Studies by Sturrock and Cathie (1980) showed that hedges were uneconomic compared with alternative forms of fencing. Advances in fencing techniques and materials, particularly the use of high tensile wire which decreases the number of stakes required, are likely to make the cost difference even greater. Economic arguments are unlikely to save hedges, but a move towards balancing landscape and wildlife against the maximization of agricultural production may do so.

PROFITS FROM HEDGEROW TIMBER?

Although hedgerow trees are often argued to be money in the farmer's pocket, the actual returns may be little or nothing. Hedgerow trees are often difficult to fell and transport. Timber merchants may not accept them, especially since these trees have a reputation of ruining saw teeth due to embedded nails, staples and bits of barbed wire. Customarily, the merchant pays for none of the wood below the offending object.

In opposition to this, Pollard, Hooper and Moore (1974, p 205) report one Wiltshire farmer who 'Claimed to make more money selling his hedgerow elms for making coffins than from the crops in the fields they surrounded.' Sadly, this shows the other side of the hedgerow tree business. As Tinker (1974) concludes, 'hedgerow timber now brings in a good enough price for farmers to fell it for the money, but not enough for it to be worth continuing to grow hedge trees as an additional source of income'.

The strongest case can be made for the production of hardwood veneers. Foresters now recognise that hedgerow trees, if properly managed, have the wide spacing and access to light which allows them to grow relatively quickly and obtain the big girths required of veneer timber. However, top quality timber must be of a minimum length, usually 7' (2134mm) of unblemished stem, ie having no wounds, faults, branches or knots. This means that advice is essential on proper management, especially pruning and protection, and that trees must never be used as fenceposts etc with the likelihood of blemishes and embedded metal.

Advice is also important before beginning any planting programme, since different sites favour different species. The greatest demand, at various times, has been for walnut, oak and sycamore. Of course, anyone planting now is planting for his successors or for the increased value of his holding on sale, and the actual economics of production varies greatly depending on taxation.

The Wildlife Value of Hedges

The widespread destruction of hedgerows has obviously eliminated a great deal of valuable wildlife habitat. Some conservationists argue that, worse, we are creating an 'ecological desert' in places such as the eastern counties where in some areas nearly all hedgerows have gone. The new agricultural landscape is an ecologically simple one. Will it be subject to the self-destructive instabilities associated with simple systems in nature? Even if, for example, hedges cannot be proved to supply enough predators to control pest outbreaks, a landscape which loses its hedges loses a large proportion of its wildlife and becomes that much less interesting.

To what extent are these fears founded? Pollard, Hooper and Moore (1974) investigated what is known about hedges and their importance to various forms of wildlife. The summary here is drawn largely from their work.

THE HEDGEROW AS AN ECOSYSTEM

Vast forests once covered most of Britain. Because of this, the country's flora and fauna, particularly its bird and insect life, is mainly of woodland origin and has had to adapt as best it can to the disruptive effects of man's clearances. These have been so recent, in evolutionary terms, that only a few birds have been able to move out from their woodland or glade homes to the new landscape of fields, parks and gardens.

Hedgerows provide a partial substitute for lost woodlands. They are essentially woodland edges without the woods, forming an 'ecotone' or border area between two other ecosystems. Ecotones often share many of the creatures of both other systems and so are doubly rich in wildlife. But hedges today are seldom backed by woods, so plants and animals which need blocks of woodland cannot use the hedge ecotone. On the other hand, those species that already preferred edge conditions have been able to dominate hedges more readily.

THE HEDGE FLORA

The most widespread hedge shrubs, such as hawthorn, blackthorn and elder, are essentially scrub plants adapted to the colonisation of open lands. Other species cannot easily seed into open land and so colonise hedges slowly if at all. When these species are found in a hedge it probably indicates a woodland origin (p 110).

In some ways it is not the shrubs but the climbing plants which really characterise hedges (p 54). The hedge manager considers them 'weeds', since they tend to choke out the shrubs, but they thrive on sunlight, support for their weak stems and an occasional cutting back, all of which the hedge or hedger supplies.

At ground level, a hedge is a relatively undisturbed place compared to the fields around it. Perennial herbs flourish here, particularly the Umbelliferae such as cow parsley (Anthriscus sylvestris), hogweed (Heracleum sphondylium) and hedge parsley (Chaerophyllum temulentum). Once again, these are species which take advantage of sunny protected locations rather than species of the deep woods. 'Woodland relic' herbs are of interest in the same way as relic shrubs (p 110).

From a management viewpoint, a narrow hedge is just as suitable to hedge flora as a wide one.

BIRD LIFE

Hedges and hedgerow trees as a bird habitat

The use which birds make of hedges is most easily shown in a table (adapted from Pollard, Hooper and Moore, 1974, p 123). The species are listed in evolutionary order, as in most field guides. The use made of each part of the hedgerow is given as N (nesting only), F (feeding only) or N/F (nesting and feeding). An asterisk

(*) after the letter indicates that the species is common in that part of the hedgerow. Those species without an asterisk may find the hedge a less favourable habitat or may be rare. (See table over page).

Managing hedges for birds

Pollard, Hooper and Moore (1974, p 125) distinguish by management seven types of hedge. Bird species and numbers tend to increase from the first to the last. The types are diagrammed below.

HEDGE TYPES
(after Pollard, Hooper and Moore, 1974)

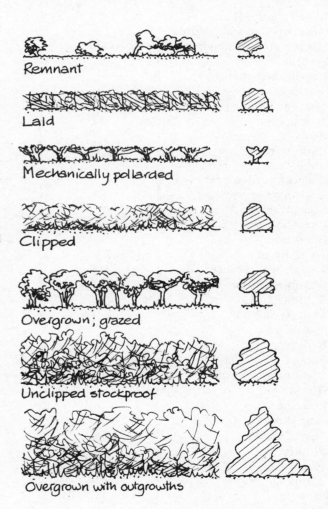

Remnant

Laid

Mechanically pollarded

Clipped

Overgrown; grazed

Unclipped stockproof

Overgrown with outgrowths

A tall hedge is generally best for birds, so if the hedge is trimmed it should be at least 4' (1220mm) and preferably 6' (1830mm) high. It is good to have as wide a hedge as possible, approaching the thicket conditions which are ideal for most of these species. In fact corner plantings of trees and shrubs are even better for birds than all but

Species	Upper branches of hedgerow trees	Trunk and holes	Shrubs	Herbs, low brambles	Ground
Buzzard	N				
Kestrel	N	N			
Red-legged partridge					N/F*
Partridge					N/F*
Pheasant					N/F*
Moorhen			N/F[1]		
Stock dove		N*			
Wood pigeon	N/F*		N/F*		
Turtle dove			N*		
Collared dove			N		
Cuckoo			N/F*[2]		
Little owl		N*			
Tawny owl		N			
Barn owl		N*			
Green woodpecker		N/F			
Great spotted woodpecker		N/F			
Lesser spotted woodpecker	F				
Skylark					N*
Red-backed shrike			N/F		
Starling		N*			
Magpie			N*		
Jackdaw		N*			
Rook	N*				
Carrion crow	N*				
Wren		N/F*[3]	N/F*		F*
Dunnock (hedge sparrow)			N/F*		F*
Grasshopper warbler				N/F	
Sedge warbler				N/F	
Garden warbler			N/F		
Blackcap			N/F		
Whitethroat			F*	N/F*	
Lesser whitethroat			N/F*		
Willow warbler			F		N/F
Chiffchaff			N/F*	N/F	
Pied flycatcher			F[4]		
Stonechat				N/F	
Redstart			F[4]		
Robin			F*		N/F*
Nightingale				N/F	
Blackbird			N/F*		F*
Redwing			F*		
Song thrush			N/F*		F*
Mistle thrush	N		F*		
Fieldfare			F*		
Marsh tit			F*		
Willow tit			F		
Blue tit	F*	N*	F*		
Coal tit			F		
Great tit		N*	F*		
Long-tailed tit			N/F*		
Nuthatch		N/F			
Treecreeper	F	F*			
House sparrow			N/F*		
Tree sparrow		N*	N/F		
Chaffinch	F*				

continued

Species	Upper branches of hedgerow trees	Trunk and holes	Shrubs	Herbs, low brambles	Ground
Bullfinch			N/F*		
Greenfinch	N/F*		N/F*	F*[6]	
Goldfinch			N/F*	F*	
Linnet			N/F*		
Lesser redpoll			N/F*		
Corn bunting					N/F*
Reed bunting				N/F*	
Yellow-hammer				N/F*	
Cirl bunting			N/F		

Notes:

[1] Especially over ditches.
[2] Lays eggs in dunnocks' nests etc.
[3] In ivy.

[4] And other species on migration
[5] And many other shrub and herb species
[6] And other shrub and ground species.

the most overgrown hedge, although any hedge is better than none.

Most birds prefer hawthorn hedges over elm and tend to concentrate in stretches of hawthorn within elm hedges. This is presumably because the thorn provides better cover, comes into leaf much earlier in the year and usually supports a more abundant insect life.

The density of bird nests in hedges seems to be determined not so much by territorial as by food limitations. One may be able to encourage a particular species to nest more heavily by providing supplementary food.

Game birds

The pheasant (_Phasianus colchicus_), partridge (_Perdix perdix_) and red-legged partridge (_Alectoris rufa_) are important game birds closely associated with hedgerows and hedged fields. Hedgerow destruction has hurt all three species, although pheasants have suffered rather less since their population can be augmented by hand-rearing.

Only _Perdix perdix_ is native to Britain, where it depends almost entirely on agricultural land. Partridges usually nest in the hedgerow verges rather than in the hedge bottoms. The width of the verges is more important than the width of the hedge, but the hedge provides necessary cover. Nesting partridges dislike seeing neighbouring pairs, so the more their sight lines are blocked by hedge shrubs the more nest territories can occur in a given area. The verges provide a vantage point with low cover and

a dry, sheltered bank to raise chicks. From the keeper's viewpoint, nests concentrated along hedgerows are easy to keep track of and ground predators can be more easily controlled.

The impact of hedge removal on hedgerow birds

Pollard, Hooper and Moore (1974, p 132) conclude that while hedges are essential for the survival of many species of birds on individual farms and in large unwooded areas of the countryside, they are not needed for the survival of species in the country as a whole. However, if the total acreage of deciduous woods and scrub were greatly reduced hedges would become much more important for bird life. This is why hedgerow destruction is particularly harmful in areas such as the eastern Midlands and East Anglia, which have already lost most of their woodlands, and in more open areas generally.

A frequent argument is that birds require hedges as corridors between suitable habitats such as spinneys and woodlands. This may have been true before the sparrowhawk was eliminated from much of Britain by gamekeepers and persistent organochlorine pesticides, but now small birds can fly cross-country with little danger. In fact, the corridor argument applies much more to small mammals, reptiles, amphibians and invertebrates.

OTHER ANIMALS

Too little data is available on the detailed effects of hedge destruction on mammals. As with birds, it seems, tentatively, that local populations suffer but that no species is directly threatened. The bank vole has declined more than most mammals, probably because it is a diurnal creature which depends on the hedgerow for cover. More than birds, small mammals may depend on hedgerow corridors linking 'islands' of more suitable habitat. The sides of overgrown ditches serve the same function.

Hedges, or rather banks and ditches, are prime locations for Britain's few species of amphibia and reptiles. Amphibia find damp places in the ditches, hibernation burrows in the banks and warming-up places in the shelter of hedges. Reptiles are more frequently seen in hedge bottoms, probably because they are larger and more active although not necessarily more abundant. Banks may be more important than hedges for reptiles. Studies of vipers in Purbeck, one of the few places in the country containing all six species of reptile in relatively great numbers, showed that they used the banks for hibernation, spring feeding and autumn nesting. Banks were also important migration routes between the dry winter habitat and the wet summer feeding areas. Hedgerow removal would seriously disrupt the life pattern of these snakes and possibly other reptiles as well.

As with birds, most British invertebrates are of woodland origin and therefore find hedges a relatively good substitute for woods. Hedge shrubs come into leaf early in the year, well before forest trees such as oak, elm and beech, and this early growth combined with early flowering provides a bonanza for spring insects. The number of invertebrates which feed on a particular shrub or tree species has been shown to relate to the length of time the tree has been part of the native flora and its relative post-glacial abundance. Oak leads the list with two hundred and eighty-four insect species followed by willow and birch. Next comes hawthorn with one hundred and forty-nine species. Other hedgerow components with many insect associates include apple (ninety-three species), elm (eighty-two), hazel (seventy-three), beech (sixty-four) and ash (forty-one). Recent introductions tend to be poor in insects, although a few natives are deficient as well, including hornbeam (twenty-eight) and holly (seven) (Hooper and Holdgate, 1968, p 55). Hedgerow shrubs are obviously important for insects, even given the species overlap between different plants. Over a hundred types of moth feed on hawthorn alone and nearly as many utilise blackthorn. The flowering herbs of the hedge bottom are also very important, with close associations with such species as the wall brown and brown hairstreak butterflies. Invertebrates which depend on hedgerow buds and flowers often suffer from late winter or spring trimming. The best hedge for invertebrates is one which is old and overgrown.

A Future for Hedges?

In 'The End of the English Landscape', Tinker (1974) argues that 'the same utilitarian forces which created the enclosure countryside are now destroying it. The best we can do is to guide these forces, and try to ensure that the power-driven landscape of the 20th century comes to contain as much beauty as the manual landscape it is replacing'. His view that 'hedges are useless' might dismay even some farmers, but he does point the way to a creative response to the fact of hedgerow removal.

The Countryside Commission report, 'New Agricultural Landscapes' (1974), explores in detail the dynamics of landscape change and gives a strategy for maintaining the amenity and wild-life value of farmland. The follow-up report, 'Agricultural Landscapes - A Second Look', details the progress of this strategy in seven study areas. The key idea is that every farm contains unproductive land which could become the site of semi-natural vegetation such as broad hedges, scrub, rough grass or thickets of trees. There are two types of marginal land:

a   Inherently unproductive land such as wet areas, steep slopes, stream banks and soil boundaries.

b   Artificially unproductive land, including ownership boundaries, awkward corners to fields or around buildings and roadside verges.

These are sites where hedges, if there are any, tend to survive. If these areas lack hedges, why not let them go back to scrub for the benefit of wildlife and amenity? The resulting landscape would lose the checkerboard effect of small enclosed fields but would emphasise major features and discontinuities by natural lines and blocks of trees and shrubs.

Most conservationists would argue that, in addition, certain hedges are well worth preserving on historical or wildlife grounds. What is needed, as Pollard, Hooper and Moore (1974, p 221) indicate, is a list of 'best' hedges which, once identified, could be protected by Tree Preservation Orders (already in existence for one hedge, but vehemently opposed by most farmers when applied in this way), subsidies or other inducements. Such a list should include:

a   Hedges with many shrub species. These
    are likely to be of both wildlife and historical
    interest.

b   Important boundary hedges, for example
    those showing Roman road alignments,
    monastic estates or ancient forests.

c   Important amenity hedges, such as those
    along foot and bridle paths or those that
    enhance the view from public access points.

d   Hedges for education, located convenient to
    schools for the teaching of local history and
    biology.

Surveys and survey procedures for finding these
'best' hedges are outlined in Appendix A.

HEDGING, A CRAFT TO CONSERVE

Most people, if they give it a thought, assume
that hedge laying has or soon will go the way of
chair bodging and charcoal burning. This must
surprise those hedgers still active, since although
few young hedgers are being recruited there is
more work to do today than there has been for
some years. Many farmers went over to
mechanical trimming after the war (virtually no
trimming is still done by hand) and thought that
never again would they have to have a hedge laid.
Now, after a quarter century of annual trimming,
their hedges show distinct signs of deterioration
which can only be halted by laying (p   61).
Gappy hedges can be fenced, but the cost of
fencing is rocketing. So, once again, the
hedger is called in to renovate these ragged old
barriers.

Despite renewed demand, hedging is in danger
of dying for two reasons. First, as already
mentioned, few young men are learning hedge
laying as a trade. Although there is room for
more, hedging like many manual outdoor jobs
lacks appeal. Also, being seasonal, it must be
coupled with another occupation. Traditionally
this has been farm labouring. Most 'professional'
hedgers were farm hands who happened to excel
at this aspect of their work and so were
encouraged to do as much of it as possible.

This brings up the second and related problem.
Modern farming is too mechanised to provide
opportunities for workers to learn hedging as
part of their job routine. Instead, tractor
driving and other mechanical skills take the
emphasis and achieve the glamour associated in
the past with skilled hand work. No longer is
there a large number of 'ordinary farm hedgers'

to supply men for local competitions, through
which the better craftsmen could achieve
recognition beyond their own farm. Competitions
and training courses tend to fail when few young
workers join them, even if public interest remains
great. Some of those that remain are listed in
Appendix B.

One hopeful sign is the renewed interest in
country crafts in general. This may spill over
to include hedging, bringing with it a wider
enthusiasm for competitions and courses and an
interest in employing craftsmen hedgers on local
work. Just as important, more people may be
willing to try the craft themselves and learn just
how satisfying it can be, whether practiced in
the privacy of one's own garden, before good-
natured public scrutiny at competitions, or in
the fellowship of volunteers working together on
tasks such as those organized by the
Conservation Volunteers.

3 Hedges and the Law

Most legal considerations apply to hedges as boundary features. Other points are concerned with the possible damage which can be caused by hedge shrubs and trees and with various problems of trespass.

Information in this chapter is from Beddall (1950) and LeSueur (1951). Certain points may be out of date or subject to varying interpretations; professional legal advice should be sought in any ambiguous or disputed case.

Hedge Ownership

a   Where a hedge has a ditch on one side, the hedge is presumed to belong to the owner of the field on whose side of the hedge there is no ditch, unless deeds state otherwise. The boundary is the side of the ditch farthest from the hedge.

b   If a ditch exists but has been so damaged or neglected that the exact edge cannot be determined, the distance can sometimes be settled by reference to local custom. The usual width allowed is 4'6" (1370mm) from the root of the hedge to the far side of the ditch. However, this 'custom of the country' may not necessarily be followed by a court of law.

c   Where the hedge is ditched on both sides or on neither side, ownership is usually mentioned in the deeds. If the hedge is ditched on both sides, it usually belongs to both parties.

If the hedge is planted right on the boundary, half belongs to one man and the other half to his neighbour. The dividing line is taken vertically from the boundary line.

d   If there is a ditch on both sides or on neither side, and ownership is not clear in the deeds, it can be claimed by one party on the basis of 'acts of ownership'. These include ditching, cutting and laying, replanting or trimming, or felling and removing trees. In such cases it seems necessary to prove that the adjacent owner knew of or acquiesced in these acts and raised no objection to them. Twenty years of continual use is usually looked upon as an 'immemorial custom' conferring right of ownership.

e   Where the origin of a hedge cannot be determined and there are no acts of ownership, the hedge belongs to both owners in equal parts.

f   When land is sold the boundary may be based on Ordnance Survey field lines. These indicate the centre of a hedge rather than the true legal boundary, and to avoid later dispute the actual boundary should be determined before purchase.

Boundary Hedge Maintenance

a   The owner is responsible for repairing the hedge and clearing the ditch.

b   If a hedge exists on the boundary line, the owner of each half is responsible for trimming and repairing his half and can do what he likes with it.

c   When a hedge belongs to both parties jointly, it is assumed to be divided down the middle and each party is responsible for maintaining his half.

d   When digging or clearing out a ditch along a hedge, the owner must not cut into his neighbour's land. He must throw all soil upon his own land. The same applies to hedge trimmings.

e   If any poisonous hedge trimmings or plants are cut and left on the neighbour's land and the neighbour's cattle eat them and die, the neighbour can claim damages from the owner of the hedge. But if the stock reach through to eat cuttings on the hedge owner's side, the owner of the stock has no claim.

f   The owner of a ditch can erect a fence at its edge, along the boundary line, to protect his ditch. He is then responsible for repair and maintenance of the fence.

Obligation to Fence

a   There is no law to compel a landowner to hedge or fence his land. But if he fails to do so he cannot claim for any damages from the owner of straying stock, etc.

b   Railways, however, must fence against cattle belonging to owners or occupiers of land adjoining the railway, to prevent them from straying on the line. The railway company is liable for damages to stock due to improperly maintained fences.

c   Each man is responsible for his own trespass and that of his stock. So while he is under no obligation to fence in order to keep out his neighbour's stock he must prevent his own from straying on another's land. He cannot claim for damages if the cattle stray and injure themselves on a neighbour's ditch or hedge.

d   If the hedge between two neighbours is defective and only belongs to one occupier, the other neighbour must fence in order to control his own stock. He can put up any sort of fence but it must be on his own land.

e   Where a hedge is owned jointly and it is defective, the owner of stock can place the fence in the hedge itself, along the boundary line.

f   An owner or rent-paying tenant can claim damage done to his fences, hedges or gates by any trespasser, including a Hunt.

Branches and Roots

a   The owner or tenant of any land is entitled to cut off branches which overhang or roots which penetrate from his neighbour's hedge, as long as he does it on his side of the boundary. The boundary is presumed to run vertically up and down from the line at ground level. He cannot claim expenses from the owner.

b   Cuttings remain the property of the hedge owner. The neighbour who cuts off overhanging branches cannot utilise them in any way. However he can place all cuttings on the owner's land. If the owner throws them back, the neighbour can claim for any financial loss incurred.

c   If he has to enter the owner's land to cut off overhanging branches the neighbour must first serve notice that he intends to do so. The owner can then do the work himself if he wishes. Otherwise he cannot prevent the neighbour from entering his land unless he obtains an injunction. However, he can claim for any damages resulting from the neighbour's entry on his land.

d   The neighbour must exercise every care to do no injury to the hedge or overhanging trees when lopping off overhanging branches or penetrating roots.

e   A neighbour has no legal right to any fruit borne upon overhanging branches. If he can show that he has enjoyed the privilege of picking overhanging fruit, based on the present or previous owner's consent, the owner cannot withdraw the privilege.

f   The owner of the fruit may, with his neighbour's permission, enter his neighbour's land to pick any fruit from overhanging branches or pick up fruit which has fallen from these branches.

If he is refused permission to enter and his neighbour refuses to deliver to him any fallen fruit, then the owner is justified in entering without permission. But he must not use force, nor must he do any damage, even to the extent of trampling on dug soil, or he can be sued for trespass.

Tenant and Landlord

a   The upkeep, maintenance and repair of hedges, ditches, etc is usually the tenant's obligation. In many cases the landlord must provide the necessary materials for the work. This should be stated clearly in the tenancy agreement.

b   In most cases the tenant cannot remove hedges or fill in ditches without the consent of his landlord.

c   All timber, trees and saplings belong to the landlord.

d   All bushes belong to the tenant.

e   Windfall timber belongs to the landlord, though in some districts local custom gives the tenant the right to the loppings.

f   Any decayed or dead timber or trees which are not timber when blown down belong to the tenant.

'Timber' means trees which are fit for building and repairing of buildings. 'Oak, ash and elm of seventy years growth are in all places timber, and other trees are timber by custom of the country. '

Nuisance

'Nuisance' is defined as something that may cause injury, damage or inconvenience to others.

a   The owner is not liable for accidents caused by falling trees unless he knew or ought to have known that the tree was dangerous.

It can be argued that he should know that certain trees are likely to be dangerous, for example shallow-rooted trees such as elm and ash which, if growing near a ditch or on a bank, will be anchored mainly by the roots running away from the ditch or bank into the field.

b   The same thing applies to hedge shrubs, hurdles or fencing placed in the hedge etc. The owner can be sued for damages if he should have known that these would be likely to cause injury by reason of their condition.

c   The owner of a roadside hedge or a hedge beside a public footpath is responsible for seeing that the hedge does not become a nuisance.

If the hedge overhangs, or obstructs road signs or lighting, he must trim it back. If any portion of the hedge, bank or hedgerow trees fall on the right of way he must remove it. If he does not do this and the public is forced to make a detour through his land, he cannot claim any damage from their doing so.

d   No tree, bush or shrub may be planted within 15' (4.6m) of the centre of a road. Highway authorities may oppose the planting of trees within 15' of the carriageway on major roads and 12' (3.7m) on less-used rural roads (Countryside Commission, 1974, p 52).

4 Safety and Equipment

The following safety and equipment lists are basic to all aspects of hand hedging work. Powered equipment is not included here but is mentioned where appropriate in later chapters. Machine work requires protective clothing and safety equipment additional to that which is listed below.

Hedging and fencing materials such as stakes, binding and wire are described where appropriate in the text.

Safety Precautions

a Have a suitable first aid kit on hand at the work site (see below).

b Take care with billhooks, slashers, axes and saws. Remember that they are edged tools and are safest when sharp. Billhooks in particular must be razor sharp to cut pleachers cleanly and without dangerous effort. Keep a safe distance from other workers when using edge tools: at least 7' (2.2m) for billhooks and axes, 8'-9' (2.5m-3m) (twice the tool length) for slashers.

c Do not use a power saw unless you have been trained and are sure of the particular safety requirements of this machine.

d Do not work in soaking rain. Once gloves, tools, the ground and the trees become wet the dangers of slipping and hurting yourself become too great.

e Wear suitable tough clothing (see below). Thorns and bramble picks are a constant hazard. Most vulnerable are hands and wrists, followed by knees and face. If you sometimes wear glasses it is best to work with them on as a precaution against jabs in the eye.

Attend to splinters promptly. Don't ignore even the smallest - they can cause serious infection. Go to a surgery immediately for emergency treatment if you have any serious pain or swelling. There is no point in being stoical about this.

f Be careful with the fire if you are burning trimmings. Build it downwind of the hedge and a few yards from it. When you can, it is best to build it on the far side of the ditch or on a footpath or towpath.

Keep it small and well packed down. Make sure that someone equipped with a pitchfork is responsible for watching over it at all times. Do not leave the fire until it is down to embers and you are certain that it will not spread.

g Keep tools and equipment out of the way of cattle - they are liable to be mistaken for fodder! Cows and bullocks have an insatiable interest in fires; the best fire tenders are repulsive and capable of bellowing.

Clothing

The aim is always safety and comfort first.

a Overalls or close-fitting work clothes. Loose clothing is a hindrance particularly when laying a hedge. Wear only old clothes which won't be ruined by a few holes.

b Boots. Heavy leather work boots with spiked or deep moulded soles are safest. Wellingtons may be necessary when cleaning a ditch or working in wet conditions but avoid wearing them when hedge laying. They are too slippery.

c Gloves or mitts. These are essential when handling thorns and brambles. Garden gloves or ordinary leather work gloves are not suitable for hedge laying as the thorns go through them. Good quality hedging gloves or mitts have long gauntlet-style cuffs to protect the wrists, and are made of single pieces of chrome leather, sewn with thick thread. They cost about £23.00, and suppliers include W G Todd and Son, Rannock House, Crescent Green, Kendal, and The Smithy, New Invention, Bucknell, Shropshire. The BTCV supply a range of much cheaper gloves and mitts which are suitable for most volunteer use. Mitts cost £3.75, and gloves cost £1.72 (all prices 1984).

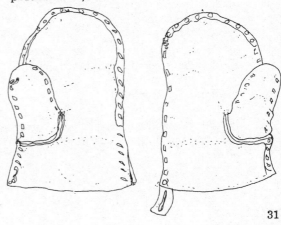

d   Heavy leather knee pads with elastic or rawhide straps. Sewn-on leather patches are usually inadequate to prevent splinters when kneeling.

e   Hat. Keep your prize deerstalker on the peg. An old cloth or leather cap is better, to minimize scalp wounds when hedge laying.

Tools and Accessories

This list is for the individual worker. On group planting or turfing tasks there should be spades or shovels to go around. The same applies to billhooks on group trimming or laying tasks. Other tools should always be within easy borrowing distance of every worker.

FOR ALL TASKS

a   First Aid Kit. Keep this with you at all times. The BTCV can supply standard first aid kits which comply with the 1981 Health and Safety Regulations (First Aid). For six to ten people, the contents are:

   1 guidance card
   20 individual sterile adhesive dressings
   2 sterile eye pads with attachments
   2 triangular bandages
   2 sterile coverings for serious wounds
   6 safety pins
   6 medium size sterile unmedicated dressings
   2 large size sterile unmedicated dressings
   2 extra large size sterile unmedicated dressings

   From experience on tasks, the following are also found to be useful:

   4" (100mm) crepe bandage
   tweezers
   scissors
   insect repellant
   antihistamine cream for insect bites
   sunscreen cream
   mild antiseptic cream
   eye lotion and eye bath

   A list of local hospitals with casualty departments should also be to hand.

b   Spade or Devon shovel

c   Mattock or digger. (Spades, Devon shovels, mattocks and diggers are discussed further below.)

PLANTING: ADDITIONAL EQUIPMENT

a   Garden fork or five-tined cultivator

b   Trowel, for transplanting small seedlings.

c   Sharp knife, for cutting back long roots and damaged fibre.

d   Twine, for lining out the hedgerow.

e   Stakes or poles, for marking the hedgeline and position of plants.

f   Rule or stick cut to length for setting out plants at the correct distance.

TRIMMING, CUTTING AND LAYING: ADDITIONAL EQUIPMENT

a   Billhook

b   Axe

c   Slasher or longhandled hook. (Billhooks, axes and slashers are discussed further below.)

d   Bow saws. The small triangular 21" (533mm) saw is especially useful in confined conditions. Carry a 30" (762mm) saw for larger material unless you take a chain saw. See page 31 for a note on the use of the chain saw when hedge laying.

e   Mallet, sledge hammer, mell or wooden billet, for knocking in stakes.

f   Sharpening stones. Slashers and hooks are best filed with a cylindrical stone. Axes need a flat, circular stone. Use either type on a straight-edged bill.

g   Flat file, for taking out nicks in edged tools. Carry one with you unless it is more convenient to do major sharpening in a workshop at day's end.

FIRES: ADDITIONAL EQUIPMENT

a   Matches

b   Solid fuel fire lighter or container of paraffin

c   Pitchfork

FENCING: ADDITIONAL EQUIPMENT

Fencing will be the subject of another publication

in this series. The <u>minimum</u> additional equipment needed for short-lived unstrained fences such as those mentioned in the text (p 52) includes:

a   Crowbar

b   Wrecking bar ('swan neck')

c   Claw hammer

d   Fencing pliers

OPTIONAL EQUIPMENT FOR SPECIAL SITUATIONS

a   Gorse hook or other short-handled hook, sometimes used as a trimming tool by Welsh hedgers (see below).

b   Shears. Useful for trimming garden or other hedges where neatness is all-important, but slow to use.

c   Secateurs. Needed only for final trimming in Welsh hedging competitions.

d   Crook. Some Welsh hedgers use a short crook cut from a hedge or coppice to help hold branches out of the way when trimming. It is especially useful when cutting gorse hedges, used in combination with a gorse or furze hook.

e   Boards or mats, used only in West Country competition turf hedging. These are laid over the turf so that it is not trampled during work.

Choosing Cutting Tools

Billhooks, axes, slashers and miscellaneous cutting tools came in a wide assortment in the past, before the amalgamation of the edged tool industry into a few big firms. These companies have standardised local tool types and are gradually reducing the selection. Nevertheless the choice is still quite varied and some guidance may be helpful, especially because general utility hooks etc are not necessarily the best for the rather specialised task of hedging. Your local ironmonger may not carry types traditional to other parts of the country. He should, however, have the catalogues of major manufacturers. Carriage costs raise the price of specially-ordered tools so combine orders when possible to minimise the expense.

BILLHOOKS

Every county, and some areas within counties, once had their own type of billhook. Today, with hedge laying restricted mainly to the Midlands and Wales, it is billhooks from these areas which are most often used by hedgers.

<u>Regional preferences</u>

Midlands hedgers are strongly loyal to the 'Leicestershire' or 'Warwickshire' billhook. This is a one-handed tool with a fairly short handle. It combines a curved billhook edge and a shorter, straight edge.

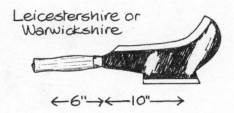

Leicestershire or Warwickshire
←6"→←10"→

Most craftsmen use the curved side for general and heavy cutting and reserve the straight blade for final trimming, topping of stakes and other light work which will not damage the razor edge. A few workers develop a preference for the exclusive use of one side or the other. Some Midlands hedgers use the Yorkshire billhook, a similar but heavier, longer-handled tool which can be used either one or two-handed.

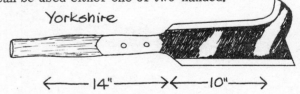

Yorkshire
←——14"——→←——10"——→

Welsh hedgers use a far greater variety of billhooks than those from the Midlands, but they share the common trait of <u>not</u> using the Leicestershire or Warwickshire type, although a few use Yorkshires. Welsh bills are single-edged. Many Welsh hedgers carry two or three of varying weight, the lighter of which are known as 'hackers'. Most of these tools have a somewhat curved edge but some, particularly the lightest, may have a straight blade (See diagrams next page.)

The 'hedge grip', the notch at the end of the Llandilo's blade, is a feature of west Wales billhooks (and those from a few other, scattered parts of the country). It enables the workers to push and prod pleachers and brash into place using the billhook rather than hands.

South Western hedgers usually use billhooks designed primarily for other woodland work. They

Llandilo, Carmarthenshire

9" 10"

Hertford

Knighton, Radnorshire

Newtown, Montgomeryshire

prefer single-edged types varying from heavy-duty brashing models with a weighted nose, to unweighted coppice hooks, to the small, light spar hook.

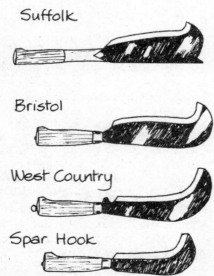

Suffolk

Bristol

West Country

Spar Hook

Tool sizes and handles

Billhooks were once made by the local blacksmith to the user's specifications. Now sizes, like blade types, are standardised and both are indicated by numbers stamped on the blade. The size number is the length of the blade in inches, measured from the top of the ferrule or socket to the extreme end of the blade. Most hedgers use number ten billhooks, ie having a 10" blade.

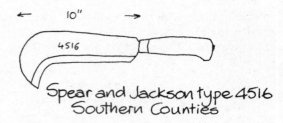

10"

4516

Spear and Jackson type 4516 Southern Counties

Billhook handles may be round or oval or have a pistol grip. Manufacturers usually supply each type of hook with an associated handle type, as shown in the diagrams above. If you strongly prefer one handle over another you may have to use a different billhook or replace the handle yourself.

Evaluation

Probably the best hedging billhook is the Leicestershire-Warwickshire type which is well balanced, does not tire the wrist and is more versatile than a single-edged implement. Unfortunately this type is no longer manufactured. The similar-looking Staffordshire billhook is still manufactured, but is not such a well balanced tool. Neither of these types are heavy-duty tools, and an axe should be carried to supplement them.

Medium-weight hackers are the next best choice for the novice hedger. They are easier to sharpen and safer for the beginner than the double-edged types but tend to be less good for fine trimming.

The Yorkshire billhook is awkward. It is tiring to use one-handed and some people find that they must grip it so far up the handle that the end of the handle tends to rub on their wrist. If used two-handed the left hand is no longer free to control the pleacher's fall as with a one-handed tool. The blade is rather too broad for close work, and can be dangerous due to its length, hook and double edge. We met one Midlands hedger who liked the heft and two-handed potential of the Yorkshire hook but worried about the blade. Eventually he filed off the hook to make two straight edges because, in his words, 'I was afraid I'd hit myself in the head with it'.

Brashing hooks, whether one of the West Country types or the equally heavy-nosed Suffolk or Derbyshire types, are difficult to hedge with. They tend to twist in the hands and slide off the stem when cutting downwards. Their blades are rather wide in the 'shoulder' for light trimming work.

34

AXES

Axe preferences follow individual rather than regional lines. We have seen a variety in use, ranging from the 7lb broad-bladed English felling axe to a short-handled 2¾lb wedge or Canadian type. Highly skilled hedgers are able to use even the heaviest axe faultlessly and ambidextrously. However, heavy large-headed axes are tiring and awkward for beginners. They are hard to use in close quarters and the result is unbalanced cutting positions and wasted or dangerously deflected strokes.

For beginners we recommend a 2¾lb or 3lb Canadian type axe with a 2'6" handle for most hedging work. This can be used one-handed, once the initial pleaching cut has been made, leaving the other hand free to guide the pleacher down. This small axe should be supplemented, when dealing with thick stems, with a heavier axe or bow saw, since it is slow to use by itself on larger trees.

For more skilled workers, or as a second axe to supplement the small one, a 5lb axe with 3' handle seems best. Again, the Canadian head is most efficient in close quarters.

Canadian or Wedge Axe

SLASHERS AND MISCELLANEOUS HOOKS

Long-handled two handed trimming tools come in many shapes. In the past, some districts had special 'hedge bills' for heavy trimming and topping. These had a broad blade rather like that of a Yorkshire billhook, and tended to be heavy to use. Today, most hedgers carry either a slasher or a curved trimming hook for preliminary cutting out of excess brush and for freeing the tops of tangled pleachers before laying them. The names of these tools vary from place to place, and those given in the diagrams are taken from standard tool catalogues.

Welsh Border Brushing Hook; handle 36"
blade 13"

General Pattern Slasher; handle 36"
blade 15"

Dunse Slasher; handle 28"–36"
blade 9"–10"

Heavy Double Edge; handle 36"
blade 9"

Lincoln Pattern Slasher; handle 28"
blade 10"–12"

Alford Pattern Slasher; handle 30"–32"
blade 10"–11"

Any of these tools will do, provided they are really sharp. While the intermediate types with a definite but not extreme curve are most popular, some workers strongly prefer the straight-bladed or reversed-curve types. In our experience a curved blade is best for the rather heavy trimming done before and during the hedge laying while the straight or reversed-curved types are handiest for light annual trimming or brushing-back.

In Wales some hedgers carry short-handled hooks for use as trimming tools. These again come in many varieties and under many catalogue names but are generally referred to by Welsh hedgers as 'gorse hooks' or 'furze hooks'. These tools seem to get little use on the average hedge, although they may be helpful for final trimming or light annual brushing of trimmed hedges as well as for cutting gorse. The hooks shown below are named as in standard tool catalogues.

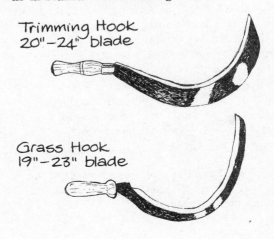

Trimming Hook
20"–24" blade

Grass Hook
19"–23" blade

Choosing Digging Tools

The choice of digging tools, as with cutting tools, depends on how much one wants to specialise. Diggers and Devon shovels, although they have other uses, are designed first and foremost for banking and turfing. Mattocks and spades are all-purpose grubbing and earth-cutting implements.

MATTOCK OR DIGGER?

The ordinary mattock is largely replaced by the 'digger' in the southwest. This grubbing tool has the mattock's broad blade but lacks the pick or root-cutting blade. In some districts the digger is itself termed 'mattock' while the double-bladed tool is called 'twibill'.

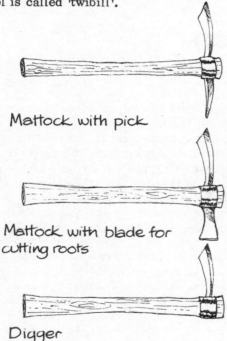

Mattock with pick

Mattock with blade for cutting roots

Digger

In hedge laying either tool can be used to expose the base of the pleachers, especially when 'laying from the root'. They also are useful when cleaning out ditches. In banking and turfing they are used to cut down damaged sections of bank and to widen out gaps to be repaired as well as to grub out stumps and roots of shrubs from the bank sides. They are also used for tamping the earth fill which forms the bulk of the bank under the 'skin' of turfs. On high banks the digger is the better tamper since the mattock is awkwardly heavy and has to be used sideways-on: (See diagram top of page).

In either case keep the tool's handle low to the bank so that the head doesn't dig into the earth but instead compresses it.

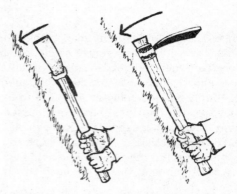

A stout stick can be used for consolidating fill if you don't need to do any grubbing and so don't want to carry either of these tools.

SPADE OR DEVON SHOVEL?

These are the basic turfing tools and are often used alone, especially on low banks where not much grubbing is needed. In Wales special turf knives formerly were used to cut and lift the sods - their curved blades were sharpened on the outer edge and cutting and lifting were carried out in the same motion. Now these have disappeared from use to be replaced by the ordinary spade. The spade is adaptable and especially suited to lower banks where turfs do not have to be lifted above waist height. On high banks, though, the spade is tiring to use and turfs tend to slip off the nearly flat rectangular blade. The blade should be kept clean and sharp to make cutting easier.

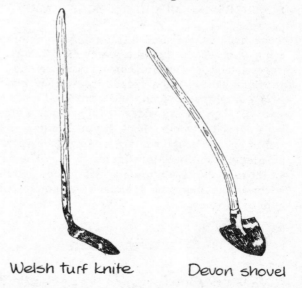

Welsh turf knife   Devon shovel

In the South West the 'Devon shovel' (in Cornwall just called the 'shovel') combines the functions of spade and shovel. This tool has a long handle or 'shovel stick', usually curved, and a triangular slightly bowl-shaped blade. Blades come in three sizes; the smallest size is best for banking and turfing. The blade is thin and is kept sharp through use, but is filed if it becomes burred by stones.

Most craftsmen cut their own shovel sticks according to personal preference. The usual length is such that with the point of the shovel touching the ground the end of the stick comes to the user's chin. Homemade sticks for diggers as well as shovels are often of willow, which is soft, light, resilient and 'plum to handle'. Ash can be used although it is rather hard. Hazel, which tends to split, is a third choice.

The Devon shovel's balance is determined by the curve of the stick and the angle at which the stick joins the blade. With the correct curve, the shovel comes down in a position for digging no matter how you turn it in your hands. This is why straight store-bought handles are a poor substitute. The angle of the blade should allow a slight lift but if it is too extreme material slides off the blade when it is raised high up. If the angle doesn't seem right a blacksmith can alter it by bending the blade's socket or eye, whichever the shovel has.

As well as making for good balance, the long handle allows the shovel to be gripped in many different positions. The triangular blade can be pushed into the ground point first or edge first, either by hand or with the aid of the boot. (See diagrams below and top of page.)

Unlike a spade, a good Devon shovel and shovel stick is very much the craftsman's personal possession, perfectly suited to one man only. But any Devon shovel is a great deal easier to use on high banks than a spade.

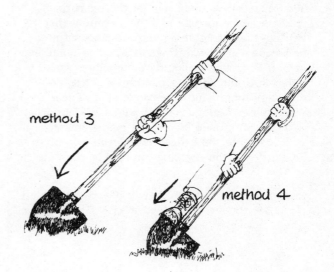

method 3

method 4

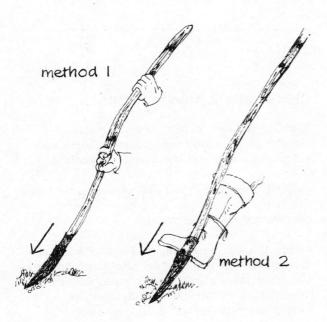

method 1

method 2

5 Planting and Early Care

This chapter outlines the characteristics of various hedge shrubs and the recommended regime for establishing and maintaining new hedgerows and hedgerow trees. The placement of new hedgerows should be considered in relation to the hedge's purpose and its likely effect on local wind conditions etc. These problems are discussed on pages 17-19. The rather specialised siting and management requirements for hedges near orchards are dealt with in the last section of this chapter.

Information in this chapter is based on Beddall (1950), LeSueur (1951) and MAFF (1970) except where noted.

Choosing Shrubs for the Hedge

Shrubs for farm hedges must be:

a   Stockproof

b   Quick growing

c   Long lived

d   Hardy to wind and frost

e   Able to withstand hard cutting and respond well to repeated pruning

f   Able to provide shelter if necessary and be heavily leafed from bottom to top

g   Adaptable to local soil conditions

h   Free of serious diseases or insect attack

i   Not usually eaten by animals

j   Relatively cheap

On the other hand farm hedge plants must not:

a   Require too much care

b   Smother other plants through too dense foliage

c   Be poisonous to farm animals

Throughout most of the country hawthorn is the best shrub on nearly all counts. But some other plants which are second rate on good sites come into their own under more extreme soil and climatic conditions. Therefore it is always best to study the hedges in the neighbourhood and be guided by local custom in choosing both the shrub for the hedge and the planting method.

The section following this one lists details on each hedgerow species.

SHRUBS UNSUITABLE FOR FARM HEDGES

The following table shows species which are unsuitable for farm hedges and indicates why this is so. In the case of poisonous shrubs, cut and withered shoots are more deadly than fresh ones so they must be carefully gathered and burnt after trimming if livestock are likely to find them. In any case, poisonous species should never be used in stock hedges.

Species	Poor because of weak growth	Chokes and smothers other shrubs	Poisonous
Ash	x		
Box			x
Broom			x
Buckthorn	x		
Cherry laurel			x
Cupressus			x
Elder		x	
Guelder rose	x		
Honeysuckle		x	
Horse chestnut	x		
Laburnum			x
Oak, holm	x		
Privet	x		
Rhododendron			x
Sycamore	x		
Tamarisk	x		
Wayfaring tree		x	
Whitebeam	x		
Willow	x		
Yew			x

Characteristic Hedge Plants

Plants described in this section are listed alphabetically within two groups, 'thorny and prickly species' and 'smoothwood species'.

Suitable species for planting as hedgerow trees are listed on page 56. Herbaceous 'weed' species are listed on page 54.

Where the aim is maximum floristic interest rather than a stockproof or farm shelter hedge the description of species as 'suitable' or 'unsuitable', 'desirable' or 'undesirable' no longer has relevance. In this case any

SHRUBS FOR DIFFERENT CONDITIONS

This table is limited to native species, plus sycamore which is 'near-native'. Soil and climate indications should be treated as rough guides only.

Species	Chalk and limestone	Damp soils	Heavy clay	Loamy soils	Peat	Sand/gravel	Under shade of hedge-row tree, along wood edges	Seaside	Smoke, air pollution	Windy condtions	Fast growing	Useful for gapping or replanting in existing hedges
Alder		*										
Beech	**		*	**			*		**			
Blackthorn		*	*		*			**	**	*		*2
Crab			**	*						*		
Dogwood	*				*							
Elder1								*3	*3			
Elm4			**	*	*							*2
Gorse						**5		**	**			
Guelder rose1		*										
Hawthorn	**	*	**		**		x	*	*	**	*	
Hazel	*	*		*	*							
Holly	*	*	*6	*	*		**		*		x	*7
Hornbeam	*		*	*			*		*			
Maple	*		*					*				
Myrobalan			*					*			*	
Oak			*									
Oak, holm1							*					
Rowan		*										
Scots pine					*							
Sea buckthorn								*8				
Spindle	*						x					
Sweet chestnut			*									
Sycamore1								*3	*3			
Wayfaring tree1	*											
Whitebeam1	*											
Willow1		*						*			*	
Yew1							*					

Notes:

A single asterisk (*) indicates suitable species.
A double asterisk (**) indicates very suitable species.
An 'x' indicates very unsuitable species.

[1] These species are unsuitable for farm hedges (see **previous** page).
[2] Suckers into gaps.
[3] As a screen only.
[4] Dutch elm disease is drastically reducing elm as a hedgerow species, although wych elm is less affected than other types.
[5] On the lightest soils.
[6] Not in wet clays.
[7] Survives well after hawthorn.
[8] Being invasive, sea buckthorn should not be introduced where it does not already occur.

plant found in the hedge is normally allowed to remain unless it is an unwanted alien in a native community.

Details on the propagation and nursery care of the species most frequently grown from seed or from cuttings are given on pages 46-7. Planting recommendations, climatic and soil requirements and general evaluations are drawn from written sources. These are supplemented by comments given by craftsmen in the field for the following species: ash, beech, blackthorn, bramble and briar, elm, hawthorn, hazel, holly, maple, oak, sycamore and willow. Not all hedgers have experience with all these species, and those that have sometimes disagree with each other. Nevertheless their remarks give an idea of the response of various shrubs to laying.

THORNY AND PRICKLY SPECIES

Three of these species, hawthorn, blackthorn and holly, in that order, are the mainstays of the stockproof hedge. The others may or may not be used depending on the situation.

Blackthorn or sloe (Prunus spinosa)

Blackthorn grows more slowly than hawthorn but forms an impenetrable hedge when well established Bushes reach 3'-10' (1m-3m) in height and are thickly branched from the ground, although the bases of the branches tend to be bare of thorns, making trimmed blackthorn better against cattle than sheep. It grows in the heaviest clays and stands any amount of wind and salt spray.

Some hedgers consider blackthorn even better than hawthorn for cutting and laying, since the upper part of the branches are even thornier and there is usually plenty of brash to help keep stock away from the shoots. It cuts and lays as does hawthorn, possibly even more easily, but rather than sprouting from below the cut stem as do most species it tends to send up suckers from the roots. For this reason it spreads into the fields and can soon form dense thickets if not controlled, but at the same time it is one of the best plants for filling up gaps.

Blackthorn is disliked by some hedgers because they claim the thorns are more septic than those of other species, due to the green algae which coats all woody parts of the tree including the thorns. The thorns are very brittle and tend to break off and fragment in the wound, making clean removal difficult.

Blackthorn, especially when allowed to grow into thickets, provides cover for many birds and is favoured by shrikes for their 'larder'. Blackthorn often acts as a 'nurse' for smoothwood seedlings, protecting them from grazing animals. Another use is the preparation of sloe gin from the fruit.

Bullace (Prunus insititia)

This species is a close relative of blackthorn, resembling it and indeed frequently hybridizing with it. Pure forms are found in southern and Midlands hedges, but only occasionally in any concentration. It does not develop real spines but rather short shoots which often degenerate into thorn-like false spines. It is cut and laid like other thorny species.

Brambles and briars (Rubus and Rosa spp)

Although generically distinct, these plants are managed as if they were identical. Usually they are cut out of the hedge along with other choking 'weeds'. But in regions where tree growth is stunted and haphazard they may be kept in the hedge to add extra protection. In upland Wales some hedgers weave them in among the pleachers, saying that sheep won't eat the 'picks' and therefore will keep away from the sprouting shrubs as well. In exposed parts of the South West turf hedges are occasionally crowned with dense rows of nearly pure bramble. Its advantage is that it 'keeps down and keeps thick'. In this case it is left to its own devices, since the more its stems reroot the more impenetrable becomes the barrier.

Crab (Malus sylvestris)

The wild apples or crabs make good shrubs for stock hedging, but are best used in combination with other species since they are not so impenetrable as the thorns. They are mainly found in West Midlands hedges and were apparently more common in the last century. They should not be used near fruit trees, unless sprayed each year, since they are susceptible to insect pests and diseases.

Gorse (Ulex europaeus)

Gorse, furze or whin does not make a good hedge plant but has its uses on poor sandy soil on high ground or on very dry sites such as the tops of turf hedges, where other shrubs cannot survive. It withstands extremes of wind and salt spray. Gorse should not be laid but merely trimmed, and this should be done in spring or summer as it is otherwise easily frosted. The plants soon thin at the base and when this happens they should be cut almost to ground level to start again. Particular care must be taken with fires near gorse since it burns very readily.

Hawthorn (Crataegus spp)

There are two British species of hawthorn, the midland or woodland hawthorn (C oxyacanthoides) and the common hawthorn (C monogyna). In the field the two are usually lumped together as hawthorn, may, quick, whitethorn or simply 'thorn', the ubiquitous component of stock hedges, but the distinction is of interest for although the two species hybridise they are likely to have different origins. C oxyacanthoides is found far less commonly and it or its hybrids may well indicate woodland relic hedges since it is essentially a species of mature woods. C monogyna is the true 'nursery' or 'garden quick' cultivated in large numbers since the 18th century for the 'quickset' hedges of the enclosure era and more recent plantings. Today as in the past, hawthorn plants obtained from nurseries are almost always C monogyna and not the midland or woodland hawthorn as stated by Beddall (1950, p45).

If left to grow freely, C oxyacanthoides remains a bush of less than about 30' (9m), while C monogyna becomes a real tree up to 60' (18m) tall with a well-developed crown. But for hedge management purposes the two can be treated identically. Hawthorn is undoubtedly the most useful hedging plant under the widest conditions and forms of management. It grows in nearly every soil and situation, except high elevations and under the shade of trees. It can be propagated from seed (p 46). It can be planted as close as 4" (100mm) for maintenance by trimming or up to a yard (1m) or more apart when it will still form a stockproof hedge if regularly laid. The only caution is to not plant it near apple or pear orchards since it is associated with fireblight disease in these trees. If found near them, it should be brushed each winter to prevent flowering.

Hawthorn is nearly impossible to kill by trimming, laying or even regular hard cutting. Most hedgers prefer it to all other species, since it is supple, easy to cut, tends not to break off easily and forms a good thorny hedge with gnarled brushy ends which hold in place.

Holly (Ilex aquifolium)

Holly makes the best evergreen hedge since it is sturdy and stockproof, but is a slow grower taking up to ten years to make a 6' (1.8m) hedge.

Some hedgers claim it grows out more than up, but well-grown holly can make a thick hedge up to 20' (6m) tall and 3 yards (2.7m) thick. It is especially suited to light, peaty soils but will grow anywhere other than wet clays. Holly stands shade well and is the best plant to put under trees. It is also good for gapping since it 'follows on' well from thorn.

Holly should be planted in May or September. The site should be well dug, preferably trenched and broken up to a depth of at least 2' (610mm). The soil can be improved with well-rotted manure, but if this is used it should be put in well below the root system. If the plants have been moved with bare roots rather than the usual protective ball of earth they should be trimmed back to $\frac{2}{3}$ of the original height before setting in the hedge.

Holly can be propagated from seed (p 46). It can be transplanted when up to 5' (1520mm) tall but the ideal size is 2' (610mm). Plants 2' tall should be spaced 1'6" (450mm) apart. Don't worry if the newly-planted trees lose their leaves. However if the leaves turn brown and hang on the trees the plants should be cut back and both the roots and the leaves given plenty of water.

Holly is best clipped, but can be trimmed annually with a hook. This must not be done when there is risk of frost; August – September is the best time. Tall hedges, if clipped flat on top, should be angled inward towards the top to a width of no more than 1' (300mm), to prevent snow damage. Old, neglected holly hedges with thin bottoms can often be improved by cutting hard back and putting composted soil or well-rotted manure in above the roots.

When laying holly you should treat it like other prickly species with, if possible, even more respect. Most hedgers admit that it makes an excellent barrier and shelter. It is very brittle and can be easily damaged if laid in frosts. Some but not all hedgers say that it resprouts poorly and tends to rot at the base after laying.

Myrobalan or Cherry Plum (Prunus cerasifera)

Myrobalan or cherry plum was once thought likely to supplant thorn as a hedger for farms, as it was believed to grow faster, be cheaper to raise and to be stockproof and rabbit proof. It certainly grows fast and vigorously, making a hedge in three or four years and eventually becoming a large bush or small tree up to 25' (7.6m) high. It can make a stockproof hedge although the spines are not nearly as numerous or closely spaced as those of blackthorn, and it tends to get thin at the base. But it is not cheaper to raise than thorn and it is certainly not rabbit-proof, although given the choice rabbits attack thorn first.

Myrobalan is good on a variety of soils, being said to flourish on heavy soil, limey soil and poor soils as long as they are not too dry. It prefers situations which are not too exposed but it will stand sea breezes.

Myrobalan can be propagated from seed (p 46). It is usually planted in double staggered rows at intervals of 12" (300mm) between plants and 9" (225mm) between rows. If maintained by trimming it should be lightly clipped in late July or early August and then cut back a bit in December. LeSueur (1951, p 30) and Beddall (1950, p 46) say that when it is neglected and bare at the base it can be cut back hard to regenerate and that it is easy to cut and lay. Others however, say that it does not like hard pruning and often dies out after laying.

Sea Buckthorn (Hippophae rhamnoides)

Sea buckthorn, although admirably thorny, has too open a growth pattern to make a good hedge. It is sometimes mixed with blackthorn near the sea since it stands planting right on the shore.

Sea buckthorn is highly invasive on sand dune systems in many parts of Britain, spreading both by seed and sucker. Once established it is next to impossible to eradicate and endless labour is required to keep it from overwhelming some coastal nature reserves. Planting individuals all of the same sex prevents the production of fertile seeds, but the problem of suckering remains and it is not always easy to judge the sex of seedlings. Certainly it should not be planted without prior consultation with the nearest regional office of the Nature Conservancy Council.

SMOOTHWOOD SPECIES

Smoothwood shrubs seldom make up a whole hedge except in certain soils and exposures where the thorns or holly cannot thrive. Most often they are mixed or form short lengths of a single species within a mixed hedge. When hedges are laid, smoothwood is cut out in favour of thorn if there is a choice. When needed it is cut and laid as thorn, but more densely, to compensate for the lack of thorny brash. Protection from cattle is especially important with smoothwood hedges (p 52).

Alder (Alnus glutinosa)

Alder makes quite a good riverside hedge although it does not tolerate acid peat or stagnant moisture. It stands hard cutting and laying and is rarely eaten by stock or rabbits. Alder stakes are durable even in waterlogged conditions.

Alder buckthorn (Rhamnus frangula)

Rather similar to alder in appearance and habitat requirements, alder buckthorn does not make a good hedge plant. It has no spines and is very open in habit.

Ash (Fraxinus excelsior)

Quicker growing and more thickly sprouting than the thorns, ash is disliked for these reasons when it competes with other trees. Stockproof hedges of pure ash do exist but must be maintained by frequent laying. When possible it is best to cut it out of the stock hedge. Some hedgers say that cattle eat ash shoots more readily than those of most species. Ash is slightly more brittle than thorn, and although a softer wood it is somewhat shorter-grained. This makes it harder to cut than thorn when large.

Beech (Fagus sylvatica)

Most Midlands hedgers consider beech a garden plant, to be trimmed but not cut and laid. In Wales and the South West it often occurs inter-mixed with other trees and in these regions it is treated as they are. In some areas, such as Exmoor, beech is extremely important as a shelter hedge on high banks, since when clipped in late summer it retains the withered leaves and loses them only just before the buds burst the next spring.

Beech thrives on sand, chalk or limestone but will grow anywhere that is well drained. It tolerates high altitudes and exposed situations, another reason for its importance as an upland hedge plant, although spring frosts can damage the young foliage. It is not a good stock barrier, especially since stock eat it, and it is liable to spread widely unless kept closely trimmed or laid. However, with careful management it can be kept narrow at the base and grown to any height up to 15' (4.5m) or more. Beech is fairly shade tolerant but is not very successful in smoky conditions.

Beech can be propagated from seed (p 46). It should be planted in two staggered rows at 15" (375mm) intervals between the plants and 8" (200mm) between rows. Never cut it back hard, but weed the new hedge and prune the straggling side shoots for two years after planting. After this it should be clipped in the usual way to encourage a second growth of shoots for denser foliage. The best time to trim is July since later trimming may result in winter frost damage. For a really dense hedge the annual growth should be kept under 6"-8" (150mm-200mm) in height, and to achieve this the longer leaders should be pruned even with the shorter ones.

Beech wood is hard, tight-grained and slightly brittle, but it splits cleanly and is quite a good layer. Where survival is difficult beech becomes twisted and gnarled, and this improves its qualities as a hedging shrub since it stays tight and retains more brush around the stem.

Box (Buxus sempervirens)

Box is a small evergreen shrub, seldom growing over 10' (3m) high, found wild in a few scattered places on chalk and limestone in southern England. It is widely grown as a garden hedge plant, but is poisonous to stock and so should never be used in farm hedges.

Broom (Sarothamnus scoparius)

Broom is locally found on heaths and other sandy places particularly in the east of Britain. It is tolerant of poor soil and is sometimes sown on railway embankments and other unstable slopes to prevent landslips. It is frequently planted to provide food for game, but has no value as a barrier and, being poisonous, should never be used in farm hedges.

Cherry laurel (Prunus laurocerasus)

Cherry laurel is a long-established non-native species locally abundant as a shrub or hedge or as a widely-spreading undershrub in woods. In the far west it occasionally grows to 45' (14m). Its trimmings are poisonous to stock and so it should never be used in farm hedges.

Cupressus or true cypresses (Cupressus spp)

Various species of cupressus and its hybrids, none of them native to Britain, are widely found in parks and gardens both as evergreen hedge plants and as large specimen trees. They are hardy and fast growing and are particularly abundant near the coast in western areas, but because they are poisonous they should never be used in farm hedges.

Dogwood (Cornus sanguinea)

Dogwood is a very common plant of chalk downs. It also grows well on soils of the Old Red Sandstones. It makes a dense, tough, shrubby hedge, but suckers to form small thickets and quickly seeds into abandoned pastures. For this reason it is a 'weed' of many downland farms and nature reserves where it is controlled as much as possible. The red spring twigs and the autumn foliage are attractive and birds enjoy the berries. The wood is very hard and was once used for skewers, toothpicks and other small turned objects. It can be propagated from cuttings (p 47).

Elder (Sambucus nigra)

Elder grows very quickly, up to 4' (1220mm) a year compared to 1'6" (450mm) or so for thorns. Because of this and its dense foliage it quickly outcompetes neighbouring plants and is a farm hedge 'weed' which should be rigorously grubbed out, although it always seeds back in again. Near the sea and in exposed uplands it can be used as a screen. Cattle rarely eat it, but its berries make a lovely wine.

Elm (Ulmus spp)

Elm is frequently an important component of Midlands hedges. It stands hard cutting and regenerates freely from suckers. In fact, species other than wych elm (U glabra) are likely to spread only by suckering. This habit makes it very useful for filling gaps, which is why it often forms considerable, nearly pure lengths of hedge. Elm prefers a heavy soil and will not grow where the soil is thin. It withstands salt winds and makes a good screen tree on the coast.

The disadvantages of elm are first, that it has an extensive root system which robs moisture and nourishment from the adjoining field headlands and second, that it is subject to Dutch elm disease. Although the beetles which spread the disease most often attack large, mature trees, the disease can pass through the interlinked root systems of adjacent trees and so wipe out an entire hedgerow. Wych elm seems somewhat less prone to attack than other forms.

Elm is reasonable for laying but is not preferable to other species. Its advantage is that it is slightly 'leathery' and tends to 'hang on' rather than to break off under the weight of the cut pleacher.

Hazel (Corylus avellana)

Hazel is a good hedge plant on chalk and the drier soils where it grows strong and sturdy. Once an important coppice shrub, its pliant stems were used for a variety of products including heathering, pea sticks, hurdles and wattles for houses.

Coppicing is still the best form of hazel management where a stockproof hedge is not needed. The shoots are mostly straight with little side branching so the growth quickly becomes open and ineffective against stock. When it is laid for stock fencing it should be pleached densely so that the laid hedge is firm and tight, and the treatment should be repeated more frequently than for other hedging plants. Hazel should not be top-cut when it starts to thin at the base since this has little effect on its straight upward growth.

Hornbeam (Carpinus betulus)

This is a good hedge plant which could be used more often. It stands a variety of situations: clays and loams but not thin soils; according to LeSueur (1951, p 29) it favours heavier soils; and Beddall (1950, p 45) says that it thrives on well-drained sand or gravel soils. In many ways it resembles beech, but can be distinguished by its serrated leaves. Its advantages over beech are that stock do not eat it, and that it is frost proof. On the other hand, it is less strong due to its more pliant stems and it provides rather less shelter. Hornbeam withstands hard cutting, grows well under dense shade, has few natural enemies and makes an excellent firewood.

Hornbeam should be grown and planted as is beech. Trim it in late summer for it to retain its dead leaves until March. If planted at a rate of 1 hornbeam per 6 thorns, it breaks the monotony of the leafless winter hedge and the hedge becomes more stockproof.

Hornbeam hedges can be kept low or grown into tall thin screens for hops or fruit or to provide shade. In Germany it is often trained so that the plants cross one another at a 60° angle. The bark is cut away where the stems touch and the stems are bound together. Neither stock nor people can get through the grafted one-piece hedge.

Horse chestnut (Aesculus hippocastanum)

Horse chestnut is sometimes found in mixed hedges but usually should be cut out. It grows too openly for a stock barrier and tends to smother and shade out other shrubs.

Laburnum (Laburnum spp)

Laburnum is a small non-native tree very commonly planted in parks and gardens for its foliage and bright yellow flowers. It seeds itself freely and is often found along roadsides. All parts of the tree are poisonous so it should never be used on farms. Children should be warned not to eat the fruit.

Maple (Acer campestre)

Field maple is common in the south and west, a tough shrub which grows to 25' (7.6m) if left uncut. It withstands salt air. It is usually found singly among other hedging shrubs, since it does not make a stockproof hedge when clipped unless mixed with other species. It is reasonable to cut and lay but is very hard and brittle.

Oak (Quercus spp)

Oak is usually found as a hedgerow tree but its seedlings may survive in the hedge and come to be managed like other species. It cannot stand spring frosts and should be kept away from orchards since it is a host to a number of insect pests of fruit trees. Oak stakes are the best for hedging. As for live pleachers, oak is soft and easy to lay, a 'nice' tree.

Holm or evergreen oak (Q ilex) makes a good evergreen screen and tolerates shade, but is hardly useful for farm hedges due to its weak, open growth.

Poplar (Populus spp)

Some of the poplars make good screen trees although not used for hedges in the strict sense. They can be propagated from cuttings (p 47). White poplar (P alba) is very hardy, grows well in sandy soils and doesn't mind salt spray. In these conditions it sends out quantities of suckers which make it all the better as a coastal screen. It should be lopped at 6'-8' (1.8-2.4m) to stay thick and hedgelike. Lombardy poplar (P nigra italica) makes a good single or two-line shelterbelt at lower elevations. It holds its lower branches well, even when grown very tall, and it can be topped to form a very high hedge as in the hop garden screens of Kent.

Pine (Pinus spp)

Certain pines make good narrow shelterbelts or screens, although they cannot be considered for stock hedges. Scots pine (P sylvestris) is occasionally used in drier conditions as a rough rapid-growing farm hedge, but it does not stand salt air. It should be set out as twice-transplanted four year old trees at 2' (610mm) intervals. Therafter it can be pruned by cutting back the annual shoots to $\frac{1}{3}$ of their full length. This encourages side branching and keeps the trees compact. If a branch must be shortened it should always be cut back to a bud in the centre of a branch whorl. Austrian pine (P nigra var austriaca) and Corsican pine (P nigra var calabrica) are also useful screen trees, especially in very dry conditions, on high chalk downs or limestone hills or near the coast (both types withstand salt). Austrian pine probably makes the best single-line windbreak, but a common problem of all pines is their need for light and their tendency to thin at the base. For this reason they are best put back of an overgrown hedge which forms a skirt for the pines.

Privet (Ligustrum ovalifolium)

Privet is not strong enough to make a farm hedge by itself but it is suitable when mixed with thorns. It is evergreen and stands heavy and frequent clipping, as well as air pollution, which is why it is so common in towns. Actually this species is Japanese privet; the wild privet of England's southern chalklands , L vulgare, is less closely leaved and not a true evergreen.

Purging buckthorn (Rhamnus cathartica)

This shrub looks rather like a spineless spindle tree and may be found in hedges on chalk soil, although not useful for fencing purposes.

Rhododendron (Rhododendron spp)

Rhododendron is a long-established non-native evergreen shrub, very common in parks and gardens and once widely planted for game cover. Conservation volunteers know 'rhody' as a tenacious 'weed' of many woodland nature reserves. It occasionally occurs in woodland edge hedges and is very brittle to lay. Being poisonous it should never be used in farm hedges.

Service tree (Pyrus torminalis)

Wild service is rare in hedges in chalky soils in the South East. The ripe fruit is edible and was once sold in Kentish markets as 'chequer-berries'.

Snowberry (Symphoricarpus racemosus)

Snowberry is a thin bush 3'-5' (1m-1.5m) high. It grows wild in North America but has spread into English woods from gardens where it is often planted. It is too weak for farm hedges.

Spindle tree (Euonymus europaeus)

Spindle is a winter host of the beet and bean aphis and so should be cut out or sprayed where these crops are grown. It is an attractively coloured shrub, and its pink and orange fruits are sometimes sold as winter decorations.

Sweet chestnut (Castanea sativa)

Sweet chestnut is rarely found in hedges although it could be used on well-drained soils. Chalk and acid soils, however, do not suit it. It is indirectly important to hedges as its coppiced timber makes durable stakes.

Sycamore (Acer pseudoplatanus)

Sycamore has many of the characteristics of ash but is hardly useful as a hedge shrub because of its spreading habit of growth. It is usually cut out of hedges to keep it from choking preferred species. Stock and rabbits eat it. It makes good firewood and can be used as a windbreak or screen tree near the coast or on exposed upland sites.

Tamarisk (Tamarix spp)

An introduced plant of sandy soils, tamarisk is evergreen with long feathery branches and scale-like leaves. It is found mainly on England's south coast but has been planted as far north as Lincolnshire. Tamarisk makes a good rough hedge, 10-12' (3m-3.6m) high, in sandy seaside locations. It is unaffected by occasional tidal floodings. Tamarisk also can be interplanted with shelterbelt trees on exposed sites.

Wayfaring tree (Viburnum lantana)

This shrub is common in hedges on chalk soils, often spreading into abandoned pastures where it grows up to 20' (6m) tall. Its pliable twigs may be used for tying, and in the past its strong bark was used to fasten pack horse bundles. However it is too weak to make a good hedge plant.

Whitebeam (Sorbus aria)

Whitebeam is a quick-growing tree of the chalk downs. It is often found in hedges but is not a good hedging plant.

Willow (Salix spp)

Willow can make a rough hedge on wet ground but is hard to make into a stockproof barrier. It is occasionally cut and laid but is even more open-growing than hazel and is easily grazed back and damaged by cattle. When laid it tends to spring out of position more than most hedging plants.

Hedgers usually cut out willow where they can, but sometimes Welsh hedgers keep it in deliberately because it regrows quickly under difficult conditions. It can be useful for filling a gap where the ground is too wet for other species. In East Anglia and other peaty areas willow is often used in windbreaks and may be cut down periodically to resprout; in these cases it is not cut and laid as for a pleached hedge. Since willow is propagated by cuttings (p 47) it is important to remove the bark from the base of willow stakes unless you want them to root and grow.

Yew (Taxus baccata)

Yew is a shade-tolerant evergreen shrub, often only 6'-10' (1.8m-3m) high but in favourable conditions growing up to 90' (27m) tall. Its wood is extremely hard, elastic and durable. The cut and withered foliage is poisonous to stock, particularly horses, so it should never be used in farm hedges.

Propagation and Nursery Care

It is generally wise to buy nursery seedlings for use in new hedges. These plants have been specifically selected for long-term viability. However, where the cost of nursery plants is prohibitive it is worth raising a few species from seed or cuttings, provided you can take the time and have adequate seed bed and nursery plots. A compromise practice is to buy two year old nursery seedlings and grow them yourself for another one or two years - these plants will probably be hardier than those taken straight from the nursery and planted in the hedgerow. In the case of beech, ordinary forest transplants may be the best idea because they take quite well and because 'hedging beech' is so expensive.

Seedlings should be three to four years old and from 1'6" (450mm) to 3' (910mm) tall, before setting out. Larger plants will have trouble surviving transplantation. Where the new hedge line is exposed or has poor soil it is best to avoid seedlings taller than 2' (610mm). There is an old belief that nursery quicks are too pampered for hedgerow conditions. This may be true, not in the case of fine strong seedlings grown in good soil, but for lush but weak seedlings which have been over-fed in the nursery beds.

PROPAGATION AND NURSERY CARE OF HAWTHORN, MYROBALAN AND HOLLY

Seed of hawthorn, myrobalan and holly, as well as many other species, must undergo 'stratification' or 'winter treatment' before they can germinate properly. Treatment time varies with the species; holly and hawthorn need at least two winters.

1   Collect the fruits or berries after they have ripened in the autumn. Mix them with double their bulk of moist sand and leave them in a heap for all the flesh to rot away.

2   In the second spring, sow the seeds in 1" (25mm) deep drills, the drills 9" (225mm) apart in a well-dug bed. If you are propagating several species having different stratification requirements, you can sow them all after one winter's sand treatment. Those species which need further treatment can be left undisturbed for another winter in the seed bed. Cover the seed bed with chicken netting to prevent bird damage.

3   Allow all the seedlings to grow for two years. Do not protect them from sun or frost but keep them carefully weeded.

4   After two years transplant the seedlings to another bed. Set them at 4" (100mm) intervals in lines 8"-10" (200mm-250mm) apart. Whenever you transplant seedlings, shorten any long roots to produce strong compact root systems.

5   After one year in the new bed, hawthorn or myrobalan seedlings, but not holly, may be cut off near the ground to encourage strong roots and a more bushy top growth. In any case keep the plants weeded for two years or until they are the right height for planting out. Holly grows slowly and should be transplanted at further two year intervals, if necessary, until the plants are tall enough.

PROPAGATION AND NURSERY CARE OF BEECH

1   Gather the seed in November. The seed should be well filled, with no sign of drying out. Note that beech produces highly variable amounts of seed from year to year. A warm summer usually causes much flowering the next spring, and unless a late frost kills the blossoms a 'mast year' follows with abundant fruit. After this there is likely to be little or no flowering for a few years.

2 Sow the seeds 1" (25mm) apart in drills, covering them to a depth of $\frac{1}{4}$"-$\frac{1}{2}$" (6mm-13mm).

3 After germination, thin the seedlings to leave about two for every five seeds sown.

4 Transplant the seedlings after two years, setting them at 6" (150mm) intervals. Allow them to grow for another two years before planting them out in the hedgerow.

PROPAGATION AND NURSERY CARE OF DOGWOOD, POPLAR AND WILLOW

Dogwood, poplar and willow species are best propagated by cuttings. This is easy to do and produces larger plants more quickly than with seedlings.

1 Cut 1 year old stems for propagation. Older wood can be used but with less success. Harvest the stems in autumn and cut the basal portions of each into 8"-10" (200mm-250mm) lengths.

2 Dig trenches 6" (150mm) deep in good nursery soil for lining out the cuttings. Put a layer of sand at the base of each trench and push the cuttings into the sand layer. Refill and tamp down the soil.

3 In the second spring after lining out, cut the stems down to 1"-2" (25mm-50mm) above ground level to produce stronger root systems.

4 Transplant the cuttings to their final position in the third winter or spring.

Planting Out

PLANTING SEASON

Hedges are best planted in the autumn. Deciduous shrubs such as thorns, beech, hornbeam etc should be planted in October or November, or any time until March as long as the ground is not frozen or snow-covered. It is safer to plant evergreens such as conifers, holly, holm oak etc either in September or in April or early May to avoid the frost risk.

PREPARING THE BED

Preparing the bed involves marking out the line of the hedge, turning over and breaking up the soil and, if necessary, improving the soil. It is always important to prepare the bed of a new hedge to break up any hard soil pan which may restrict drainage and block the plants from rooting deeply. This holds true even if the bed is to have a bank built atop it.

If the hedge is to have a ditch beside it, first prepare the bed and then dig the ditch. Otherwise the ditch will get in the way, especially if you use a machine to prepare the bed.

Marking out

Mark the hedge line carefully, making it as straight as possible given any general curves or changes of direction. If a plough is used, cut out a single straight furrow before the soil is prepared. Otherwise mark the line with a set of posts. On a long line set a post at each end first. Then have one person sight between them while directing another person as he brings intermediate stakes into line with the end posts.

Turning the soil

'Double digging' the bed by hand is described under 'Planting Methods', below. Mechanical preparation may be with a rotary horticultural tiller, a deep plough or a gyrotiller.

Rotary cultivation is usually the cheapest and most efficient method for moderate lengths of hedge where the site is neither stony nor full of roots. Rototillers can be rented from garden and horticultural suppliers.

Deep ploughing should be to a depth of 12"-14" (300mm-350mm) if possible, though this will have to be less on chalk soils. It is best to plough one way only. The ordinary method of ploughing both ways tends to leave the opening furrow unploughed, unless great care is taken, and this is right in the centre of the row where the plants will be set.

Gyrotilling uses heavy machinery which is required only where a solid pan must be broken. Gyrotilling stirs up the soil to a depth of about 18" (450mm) without inverting the soil layers.

Improving the soil

Normally it is unnecessary to fertilise the soil, but if it is very poor a good dressing of farm-yard manure should be dug or ploughed in at a rate of 12cwt (604kg) per 150 yards (136m) of hedge. Make sure the manure is well dug in and thoroughly mixed through the soil.

If manure is unavailable, substitute bone meal or a balanced inorganic fertiliser such as 'Growmore' at 3-4oz per square yard (110-140 gms per square metre). Heavy clay soils benefit from liming, using ground limestone at 4-8oz per square yard (140-280gms per square metre) or carbonate of lime at 2-4oz per square yard (70-140gms per square metre). Fertiliser or lime can be added when the soil is initially prepared, but it is best to fork it in after the digging is finished, just before the final preparation of the soil.

If the hedge line follows the position of an old hedge, you should be careful to renew the soil. See 'Planting up gaps', page 52.

SINGLE VERSUS DOUBLE ROW PLANTING. SPACING THE PLANTS

Many farmers prefer double rows for stock fencing, claiming that a solid hedge is produced more quickly than with single row planting. Most hedge layers also prefer double rows to provide adequate pleachers. However, Beddall (1950, p 61) says that single row hedges are just as stockproof since the plants can develop more evenly on both sides. Single row planting is, of course, half as costly in plants.

Recommended planting distances for some species are given under 'Characteristic hedge plants' above. In general plants should be set 8"-12" (200mm-300mm) apart in each row. Double rows should be staggered with 6"-18" (150mm-450mm) between them. The exact spacing depends on the size and type of plant, the desired width of the hedgerow and the number of plants which you can afford.

Both MAFF (1980, p 7) and James (1972, p 141) recommend double row planting. MAFF suggests staggered rows, totalling nine plants to the metre. Plants should be at 10" (250mm) intervals, with rows 6" (150mm) apart. James recommends 12" (300mm) between plants and 9" (225mm) between rows as a general rule. An exception is holly, which should be planted in single rows at a spacing of at least 12" (300mm) between plants.

Where it is intended to trim but not lay the hedge it can still be made stockproof by planting at 4" (100mm) intervals.

The table below indicates the number of plants required for a double row hedge for a variety of planting distances. About half the distance to be allowed between plants should be left at each end of the row.

Distance apart of plants in the row (in inches)	Number of plants required in a double row hedge per:			
	Yard	Chain	Mile	Kilometre
6	12	264	21,120	13,115
9	8	176	14,076	8,741
12	6	132	10,560	6,557
18	4	88	7,038	4,370
24	2	66	5,280	3,278
30	2	50	4,224	2,623
36	2	44	3,520	2,185

PLANTING METHODS

On the flat with or without a ditch

This is the most common and generally recommended practice today unless the land needs more drainage than is possible with the ditch alone.

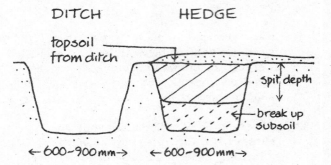

1 Prepare the bed. General points and mechanical methods are covered above. To 'double dig' the bed by hand:
   (i) Cut out a trench along the line of the proposed hedge, using a spade. Make it one spit deep and the appropriate width for the hedge, 2' (610mm) or preferably 3' (910mm). Heap the spoil to the side of the trench.
   (ii) Dig down a further one spit with a garden fork. Break up the subsoil but don't bother to lift it out. If the soil is easily worked a spade can be used instead. It is best to dig over the centre 1' (300mm) of the bed to at least 1'6" (450mm) depth.
   (iii) Refill the trench, turning over the soil to break down the lumps. Remove any weeds and roots.

2 Dig the ditch, if one is needed. The ditch's dimensions depend on the soil and on the level required to provide an even fall for good drainage. In general, the ditch should be between 2' (610mm) and 3' (910mm) wide at the top, tapering to 1' (300mm) to 1'6" (450mm) wide at the bottom, and should be 1'6"-3' (450mm-910mm) deep. The taper or

batter is important to minimise soil slump. Light soils require a more gradual batter than clayey soils.

3 Spread the topsoil thinly over the prepared strip where the hedge is to be planted. Scatter any subsoil.

4 If you break through any piped drains their ends should be replaced with nonporous pipe and a headwall built of brick, stone or concrete to hold each outfall pipe and make it easy to find it in the future.

5 Put in the plants (see below).

On top of a bank

The advantages of planting a hedge on a bank are:

a The soil remains well drained even on wet land.

b The bed is deep enough to give shrubs room to root.

The disadvantages are:

a The labour cost is higher than for flat planting.

b The soil in the bank will be poor unless care is taken to keep the topsoil on top and to renew the soil periodically.

c The plants may not stay firm in the bank.

The general method for building a bank is outlined and diagrammed below. The specialised task of building a high West Country turf or stone hedge is described in another handbook in this series, 'Dry Stone Walling' (BTCV, 1977).

1 Cut out and set aside turfs from the site of the bank and the adjacent ditch. The ditch helps drain the field and provides the material for constructing the bank. Cut ditches along both sides only if the field requires them for adequate drainage.

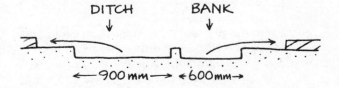

2 Prepare the bed along the line of the bank. If working by hand, first dig out the topsoil from the bank site, then fork over the second spit.

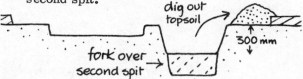

3 Dig the ditch, putting the topsoil to one side. Place the subsoil from the ditch at the bottom of the bank, building it up in layers of a few inches. Tamp each layer firmly into place. Build the bank with a batter of between 1:3 and 1:6 (p 107).

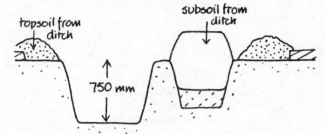

4 Replace the topsoil which you have previously set aside to finish off the bank. This ensures that the hedge shrubs will be rooted in good soil.

5 Stabilise the bank sides with turf or dry stone walling. Use the turf saved from the top of the bank and ditch and cut out more from the field headlands as necessary. See the chapter, 'Banking and Turfing', for details.

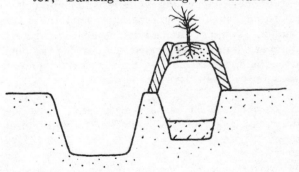

On the side of a bank or on a ledge at the foot of a bank

This method is for use on wet land where a bank and ditch are required for drainage but where, in addition, the growing hedge needs protection from strong winds in exposed situations. Only one row of plants can be placed.

Of the two variants, the hedge on a ledge takes up more room but has the advantage of keeping soil from slipping into the ditch. It is also easier to plant out. In either case the bank should be built as outlined above, with the topsoil put at the base of the bank where the hedge roots will benefit.

HEDGE ON SIDE OF BANK

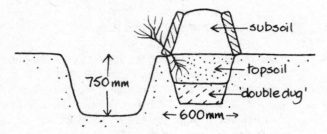

HEDGE ON LEDGE AT FOOT OF BANK

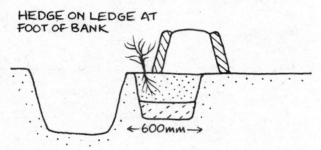

CARE OF PURCHASED PLANTS AFTER DELIVERY

Inspect the plants on delivery from the nursery. If the polythene bags which hold the roots are torn the plants are likely to be dry and, if the weather is cold, susceptible to frost damage. Soak any that have dry-looking roots in a tank of water for a few hours before planting. If the plants themselves look dry and shrivelled they should be returned. If this is not possible, soak the entire bundle. You can often revive dried-out shrubs by digging a hole in the ground and burying the plants, covering them entirely with soil. Take them out again after a few days and plant.

If you cannot plant out the shrubs as soon as delivered they must be 'heeled in' to hold them over. To do this:

1 Dig a trench long enough to take all the plants in a single line and wide and deep enough to hold the largest of the plants' roots comfortably.

2 If the plants are only being kept over for a few days they can be heeled in without undoing the bundles. For a longer period, untie the bundles and spread out the plants along the trench. They should all lean the same way, but don't worry about getting them in vertically.

3 Replace the soil to cover up all the roots.

4 Firm the soil a little with your feet. The plants should now be able to survive for months if needed before planting.

If you receive the plants during a very cold period you should wait until the frost ends to plant them out. Place the unopened bundles in a dry, frost-proof shed or cellar, where they will survive for two or three weeks if well covered with straw, sacking or newspapers. If the frost seems likely to continue for longer than this you should undo the bundles but leave the packing around the roots and heel in the bundles in a trench, if you can dig it in such weather!

PUTTING IN THE PLANTS

General rules for planting

Make sure that the plants are in good condition for setting out. See 'Care of purchased plants after delivery', above.

In addition you should:

a Put damp straw on the roots if you must leave the opened bundles exposed while planting, even for a few hours.

b Set up wind screens to protect the plants while working in cold, drying wind or frosty conditions.

c Sort the plants according to size. Do not plant large, strong individuals next to sickly specimens. If you do this the strong plants will outcompete their weak neighbours, which may die and leave gaps in the hedge.

d Cut off any damaged root fibre before planting. Cut upwards so that new roots sprouting from this point will tend to grow upwards.

e Spread out the roots as you put in the plants.

f Set the plants in at the same depth as they were in the nursery, as shown by the soil mark on the stem. Avoid planting too deep or too shallow.

g Firm the plants. The roots must be brought into close contact with the soil to do their work. In light soils firming is especially important to keep the plants steady in wind; otherwise the roots will loosen and the plants dry out.

h Irrigate after planting in dry soils, if

50

possible.

Single row planting

There are two methods. Method A is best for the lone worker. A pair of workers can use either method.

Method A: Dig out the entire trench along its length before planting.

1 Mark out the hedge line. Stretch garden or plumber's twine tightly between the stakes used to mark the ends of the hedge when preparing the soil. Steady a long line while planting by placing canes or sticks at intermediate points.

2 'Nick out' along the line. This makes it easier to dig and helps to keep the line from being displaced.

   To nick out, face the line, holding the spade vertically with the back of the blade against the line and parallel to it. Push the blade straight down to its full depth, using the foot if necessary. Do this along the entire line.

3 Dig a trench the length of the hedge, big enough to hold the largest plants comfortably, generally about one spit deep and 12"-18" (300mm-450mm) wide. Place the spoil to the side opposite the line, not on the line itself.

4 Place the plants in small bundles along the sides of the trench or lay them along it at the correct spacing, measured with a rule or stick cut to length.

5 Take up the end plant. Hold it in the trench against the end peg and the back of the trench and line. Spread out the roots. Check that the soil mark on the stem is at ground level. Push enough soil into the trench with foot or spade to hold the plant in position. Firm the plant with your boot.

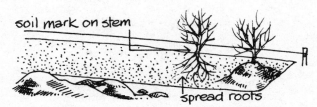

soil mark on stem

spread roots

6 Repeat step 5 for each plant, checking that the distance between it and the preceding plant is correct. Put in enough soil to hold the plants in position; do not bother to fill in the trench at this time.

7 After positioning all the plants, backfill the trench with the remaining soil, using the spade. Straighten and firm each plant as you work, sighting back along the line to make sure all plants are straight.

If two people are working together using Method A, one should hold each plant as the other fills the trench. The first person should then firm each plant. You can either fill the trench completely as you proceed or do this after all the plants are positioned.

Method B: Place the plants as you dig.

In this method two people work together, one digging out while the other holds and firms the plants.

Steps 1 and 2 are the same as for Method A.

3 Dig out only about 2' (610mm) of trench at one end of the hedge line. Follow the suggestions in step 3 of Method A.

4 The second worker should now place a plant against the end peg and the line, checking that the depth is right.

5 The digger works backward along the trench, placing the soil on the roots of the first plant. The second worker firms the plant.

6 Continue down the line. Place each plant in the section of trench opened up when the preceding plant is backfilled. To fill in the last section, bring the soil from the first length, which was placed at the side of the trench, around to the end of the hedge.

7 Check the entire hedge, straightening and firming every plant.

Double row planting

Double row planting is easiest when two people work together. Follow the same procedure as in single row planting with these modifications:

a When working alone, plant one row at a time. Plant the first row on one side of the line. Then plant the other at the correct distance on the opposite side. For a neat job, set and nick out a second guideline parallel to the first to get the spacing even between the rows. (See diagram next page.)

   This method can also be used when working in pairs.

DOUBLE ROW PLANTING : double trench

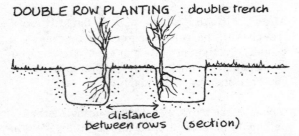

distance between rows (section)

b   An alternative method for two workers is to
    plant both rows together by digging out a
    wider trench. In this case one person holds
    two plants at a time while the other places
    earth on their roots. Place one row against
    the line and space the other by eye. Do not
    run a line for the second row since it would
    be across the middle of the trench and would
    probably break during work.

DOUBLE ROW PLANTING : single trench

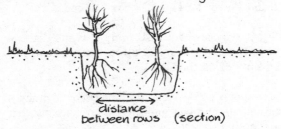

distance between rows (section)

The distance between rows must be great
enough to allow room for the roots of the
first row plants.

Planting Up Gaps

The same considerations apply to replanting gaps
in old hedges as to planting new hedges. Keep in
mind these additional points:

a   Why have the gaps formed? If because of
    poor past management or the death of
    individual weaklings, replanting the gaps
    followed by regular trimming and laying will
    be adequate. But is the hedge so old and
    decrepit that the whole thing is more sensibly
    grubbed up and replanted from scratch?
    More often, a particular length will have lost
    its vigour. In this case it is better to enlarge
    the gap by taking out adjacent poor specimens
    than to replant an insufficient length.

b   Cut out all sickly plants in and around the
    gap and grub out the stools and roots. Open
    out the gap until sound growth is found on
    either side.

c   The soil in the bed must be renewed if you
    replant with thorn. Dig it out and replace it

either with soil from the nearby field, if
this is not too poor, or with compost and leaf
mould plus a dressing of short farmyard
manure (manure containing short straw and
in an advanced state of fermentation).

When replacing the soil in a bank make sure
that the new subsoil is at the bottom and new
topsoil on top.

d   Blackthorn and holly follow on from hawthorn
    more successfully than do new hawthorn
    plants. With these species less care need
    be taken in making and manuring a new bed.
    Do not use blackthorn transplanted from the
    woods as these tend to sucker more than
    those from nurseries.

Protecting New Plantings

a   Young hedges as well as the newly planted
    gaps must be fenced on both sides against
    stock and, if necessary, rabbits and hares.
    The fence should be kept until the hedge is
    first laid, after which protection depends on
    the type of hedge. The fence need only be a
    single line of double-strand barbed wire,
    stapled to waist-high posts driven in every
    7-8 yards (7m). Set the fence about a yard
    (1m) out from the line of the hedge. Rabbit
    netting should be buried with 6" (150mm) of
    netting turned out on the field side to keep
    rabbits from digging under. A trip wire
    against hares should be placed 6" (150mm)
    above the rabbit netting.

When fencing off gaps do not nail or staple to
living wood. Bring the fence in at both ends
of the gap to stakes set near the centre of the
hedge.

b   In very exposed situations, especially near
    the coast, it may be worthwhile protecting
    the new hedge against the wind. One method
    is to erect a fence of pig netting, 4'-5' (1.2m-
    1.5m) high, along the windward side of the
    hedge. Fasten sprays of broom, spruce or
    pine to the netting to make a porous barrier.

Alternatively, put up wattle hurdles 5'-6'
(1.5m-1.8m) high, along the exposed side.
Rough hazel or willow wattles with a fair
amount of air space are best since they are
cheapest and since a porous barrier is more
effective than a solid one (pp 17-18). These
days even the roughest hurdles are likely to
be too costly for anything but amenity and
garden use, unless you have access to a

coppice and can make your own.

c   If the weather is very dry keep the new plants mulched and well watered.

d   If the ground remains wet check that the drainage ditch is functioning so that the hedge bed does not become waterlogged.

e   Weed the hedgerow for the first few years. This is especially important to prevent the early establishment of perennial 'weeds'. Later on, of course, the shrubs will withstand competition. These days weeding is usually limited to cutting back tall growth with a slasher, weeding scythe or small power mower.

Managing the New Hedge

There are various approaches to early care but in every case the aim is to obtain sturdy growth, strength and good form. Good bed preparation and careful planting ensures this to some extent. More is needed, however, especially when you want to train the hedge to a tight bushy shape for annual trimming. This can only be achieved, where the species can stand it, by shortening the leaders to promote side shooting on every plant.

Whatever the specific regime followed, it is easier to train a young hedge gradually into shape for annual trimming than to reshape it once it has 'grown away'.

Where the aim is not to trim but to lay the hedge as soon as possible it is still best to follow the suggestions below for the first year or two. Some early cutting back helps to promote new root growth as well as make for bushier plants.

A hedge designed as a screen or windbreak should be as tall and narrow as possible. Follow the same first year treatment as for other types of hedge but in later years let the leaders grow unchecked until they have reached the desired height. This may be anything from 5'-6' (1.5m-1.8m) for ordinary purposes to 12' (3.6m) or more around orchards or flower fields. Each year the sides should be clipped or brushed up to keep the growth narrow and dense.

Hedges around orchards may need additional maintenance as described later in this chapter.

THORN, BLACKTHORN AND MYROBALAN

Various authorities outline different management regimes for these species. Our experience is too limited to recommend any one in particular. Several approaches are given below.

Beddall (1950, p 67) outlines the following treatment:

1   If you set the plants out in autumn you should cut them to within 3"-4" (75mm-100mm) of the ground the following March, using a sharp knife or secateurs.

If the planting is done late in the season let them grow untouched for one summer and cut them back hard the following winter.

2   The second season weed the shrubs and the next winter cut them back along the sides with a billhook, sickle or shears. Also at this time cut back the leading upright shoots by about half their length.

3   After this let the leaders grow unhindered until the required height is reached, but cut the sides back hard at the end of each season.

LeSueur (1951, p 64) recommends:

1   Cut the plants back to a height of 2"-3" (50mm-75mm) above ground level after they have grown for one year.

2   In subsequent seasons gradually trim the plants into shape by annual cuttings with a 'switch bill' (a small light billhook), unless the aim is to lay them as soon as possible, in which case they should be allowed to grow unchecked.

LeSueur also mentions that some people cut their hedges back to the 2"-3" (50mm-75mm) level immediately after planting and then let them grow away, while others let them grow for four or five years before trimming.

MAFF (1980, p 7) suggests:

1   Leave the hedge alone during the first growing season.

2   At the end of the first season check the hedge and cut back plants which have grown away from their neighbours. Do not touch plants which are under 12" (300mm) tall but cut any straggling side shoots into line.

3   Seek local advice on later management since

this varies greatly depending on species, soil and situation. Some people say that the leaders should not be touched again until the final height is reached, which varies depending on the type of hedge. (Sheep hedges are from 3'-4' (910mm-1220mm) high, cattle hedges usually 4'6" (1370mm) and shelter hedges may be 5'-6' (1520mm-1830mm) or more.) Other people hold that the hedge should be cut back hard at the end of the second and third growing seasons and then left to grow.

BEECH, HAZEL, HORNBEAM AND GORSE

1 Just give these species a light trim after planting, cutting the leaders back by no more than one third of their height. Lightly trim the side shoots as well.

2 Repeat this treatment in autumn or winter each year until the desired height and shape is reached.

HOLLY, HOLM OAK AND OTHER EVERGREENS

Do not cut the leaders at all until they have reached the final desired height. Give the side shoots an annual light trimming to gradually bring them into shape.

Routine Care of the Established Hedge

These notes apply to annual care other than trimming, which is described in the next chapter. The suggestions are made by Beddall (1950, p 68), and repeat the practice which should be followed in preparation for laying a hedge. It seems unlikely that most land managers will be able to do this annually, as recommended, but where the hedge is laid only infrequently it is best to undertake routine care as often as possible.

The work should be done in autumn or winter.

Procedure:

1 Clear the base of the hedge, the banks and the ditches of rubbish. Grub up 'weed' species (see below).

2 Check the hedge plants and dig out any that are dead or dying. Replace these with young vigorous plants.

3 Fork in dressings of farmyard manure around the roots of any plants where growth seems poor.

4 Throw the spoil from the cleaned ditches up around the base of the plants to improve the soil.

'WEED' SPECIES

Weeds are simply plants in the wrong place. Usually they are plants which succeed all too well at the expense of other species which, for whatever reason, are deemed more valuable. Woody weeds are listed in the table on page 38 . Aside from a few tenacious shrubs such as elder, it is the climbers which present the greatest weed problem. As Pollard, Hooper and Moore point out (1974, p109) 'in some ways the climbers are the really characteristic hedge plants ... all needing support and appreciating a regular trim by a brushing hook or cutting bar'. Hard as it may seem, climbers should be grubbed out of the stock hedge before they damage it either by over-shading the shrubs or by actually choking them. Most climbers reseed readily into the hedge, so the aim is to hold them in check rather than to eradicate them.

These climbers can be considered 'weeds' of the stockproof hedge:

Bindweed (Calystegia spp)
Black bryony (Tamus communis). Also poisonous.
Brambles (Rubus spp) and briars (Rosa spp). Although usually cut out, these plants are occasionally used in the cut and laid hedge (p 40).
Clematis (Clematis vitalba), also known as travellers' joy, old man's beard and hedge feathers.
Honeysuckle (Lonicera spp)
Hop (Humulus lupulus)
White bryony (Bryonia spp). Also poisonous.

POISONOUS SPECIES

The plants listed below may require control where it is judged they pose a hazard to livestock. Poisonous shrubs and trees are included in the table on page 38 .

Poisonous plants with bulbs or corms

Autumn crocus (Colchicum autumnale) or meadow saffron. Very poisonous corm.
Arum (Arum maculatum), also known as

cuckoo pint, lords and ladies, wake
robin, and starchwort.

Poisonous trailing and climbing plants

Black bryony (Tamus communis)
White bryony (Bryonia spp), also known as
 red-berried bryony, wood vine and hedge
 vine.
Woody nightshade (Solanum dulcamara),
 also known as bittersweet.

Poisonous non-climbing plants with berries

Belladonna (Atropa belladonna), also known
 as deadly nightshade and devil's cherries.
Black nightshade (Solanum nigrum). Berry
 poisonous.
Herb christopher (Actaea spicata), also
 known as baneberry. Rare, restricted
 to the limestone area of Yorkshire and
 Westmorland.

Poisonous plants of the umbelliferous order
(Flowers in lacy umbels)

Fool's parsley (Aethusa cynapium)
Hemlock (Conium maculatum)
Water Hemlock (Cicuta virosa), also
 known as cow bane. Found in ditches.

Poisonous plants of the buttercup family

King cup (Caltha palustris), also known as
 marsh marigold. Found in ditches.
Green hellebore (Helleborus viridis), also
 known as bear's foot. Rare, on chalk.
Stinking hellebore (Helleborus foetidus),
 also known as setter wort. Found
 mainly on chalk soils.
Monkshood (Aconitum napellus), also
 known as wolfsbane. Found in a few
 shady hedges in the west and Wales. The
 black roots are the most poisonous part.

Other poisonous herbs

Foxglove (Digitalis purpurea), also known
 as thimbles and dead man's bells. Cut
 and wilted stems are poisonous to stock.
Henbane (Hyoscyamus niger). Seeds
 poisonous.

Establishing Hedgerow Trees

The pros and cons of hedgerow timber have been
summarised on page 17. Assuming that you
want hedgerow trees, the easiest way to establish

them is to keep an eye out for straight promising
saplings or 'tillers' when laying the hedge.
Tillers should be left not closer than 20-30 yards
(18m-27m) apart. Leave the tillers standing
when cutting and laying the hedge. Cut off their
lower branches and side shoots to encourage a
good crown and fewer knots in the trunk. Thereafter leave the developing trees alone when
trimming the hedge. This is easier to do for the
first few years if you trim by hand or mark out
the trees to be left before machine trimming.

Special tree tags for marking saplings are
available from many county councils, as well as
from the Tree Council. To avoid any 'unsolicited'
tagging, these are usually only distributed to
groups who already have agreement from a farmer
or landowner to carry out the work of tagging.

Oak, elm, ash, beech and sycamore are the
most frequent self-sown timber trees in England,
in the order given. In Wales the list, in order,
runs oak, sycamore, elm, ash and beech.
Conifers seldom occur, perhaps because they
cannot take hard trimming in their early years
before they top the height of the hedge. However
Scots pine, European larch, Norway spruce and
silver fir can be found occasionally.

The status of elm as 'the' hedgerow tree has
disappeared due to Dutch elm disease, and its
future is unknown. In areas where the disease
is widespread it would be unwise to select elms
over other timber species for the hedge. Suitable
species for hedgerow trees and for the replacement
of elm are listed below.

PLANTING HEDGEROW TREES

As already noted, it is easiest to wait for the
right seedlings to establish themselves in the
hedgerow. But where you want to supplement or
speed up the natural process you can plant trees
either in or beside the hedge. Both methods have
disadvantages, as explained by James (1972,
p 150), unless the trees are planted at the same
time as the rest of the hedge. Given the diffic-
ulties of planting trees in established hedges a
better idea may be to plant up waste space near
but not in the hedge. Awkward corners, steep
slopes and other 'useless' spots may support a
reasonable timber crop. The trees should always
be fenced off from grazing in their early years.

Planting in the hedge

a This is the best method if the trees are
 planted at the same time as the hedge.
 Otherwise this is difficult, impractical and

very expensive.

b   To plant in the established hedge you must first prepare individual beds for each tree by cutting away part of the existing hedge and digging a hole in the bottom. Where the hedge is well established the task may be virtually insuperable.

c   The trees planted must be reasonably large standards so that their crowns are well above the top of the hedge. This adds considerably to the cost unless you have your own nursery.

Planting beside the hedge

a   The work and cost of planting in the field or verge next to the established hedge is much less than that of planting in the hedge. However, the trees must be well protected since they are no longer shielded by the hedge itself. Erect fencing or tree guards against livestock and farm machinery if these are likely to damage the trees.

b   If the trees have to be planted on the side of the hedge with a ditch, they must be well clear of the ditch itself. But trees in this position will interfere with ditch cleaning machinery.

c   Trees beside the hedge hinder hedge cutting machines when these are operated from the same side.

SUITABLE SPECIES FOR HEDGEROW TREES

The following lists, from Beddall (1950, p 53), must be considered in the light of each species' climate and soil requirements as well as the cost of purchase and planting. It is wise to consult local experts before settling on the right tree for your hedge. Many of these trees are either cultivars or aliens and should not be planted where it is most important to retain intact the natural or native flora.

For timber

Alder	Larch
Ash	Lime
Beech	Locust
Birch	Oaks (not turkey oak)
Cedar	Pine
Cypress	Plane
Douglas fir	Poplar
Elms (field elm	Sweet chestnut
and wych elm)	Walnut
	Willow (black and white)

For firewood

Acacia	Pear
Apple	Plane
Ash	Poplar
Birch	Sycamore
Elm	and all the
Holly	Conifers
Hornbeam	
Maple	
Mulberry	
Oak	

For coloured foliage

Copper beech
Prunus pissardii

For flowers

Apples (Standards of Worcester Pearmain, Ribston Pippin, Blenheim Orange, Laxton's Superb, Lord Derby, Newton Wonder, Bramley, and Annie Elizabeth), apples for cider (Yarlington Mill, Dabinette, Sweet Coppin, Fair Maid of Devon)
Cherries (sweet, mixed for pollination)
Damsons
Mulberry
Pears (Jargonelle, Hessle, Conference)
Plums (most varieties)
Sweet chestnut
Walnut

Species suitable for replacing elm

This list is taken from the Forestry Commission leaflet, 'Replacing the Elm in the Countryside' by A F Mitchell, HMSO, 1973. As the leaflet explains, 'the most important feature of the English elm is the unique visual contribution it makes to the countryside as lines or individual trees in otherwise open areas'. While no tree can completely take elm's place to those sensitive to the visual qualities of the landscape, the trees listed below grow in similar conditions as elm and are appropriate to the open countryside. These are native or 'near native' species, ie similar or related species from nearby countries. Exotics and colour variants are out of keeping with the rural scene, although justifiable in towns and gardens.

Elm typically thrives on base-rich, moist but well-drained deep soils. These occur particularly at the edges of flood plains, in broad lowland river valleys and in gently rolling chalk and limestone areas with deep overlying soils. Some of the species listed closely resemble elm in one or more characteristics. The crown shape of oaks can look like that of some elms in winter. Grey poplar can be tall, fine boled and high domed in the crown, and suckers as does elm. Small leafed lime can have elm's crown and dense foliage, and field maple has a dense dark crown which turns a similar bright autumn yellow.

Not all the trees listed are equally suitable in every situation. Grey poplar and ash may be unacceptable on the edges of agricultural land. Ash and sycamore have great timber value but bear no resemblance to elm and so will change the scenery more than some other species. It will be difficult to establish any tree in an old hedgerow unless it has already seeded in naturally. Therefore new plantings, in field corners or near the hedge, may be the best approach to replacement of hedgerow elms.

Trees are grouped by stature as large or medium. Large trees, on suitable sites, are often 75'-100' (23m-30m) or more while trees of medium stature are seldom above 65' (20m) tall. Autumn colour is for unshaded trees in good years, and is listed only where a feature.

Species	Habit	Autumn colour	Remarks
I. Large stature			
Common oak (Quercus robur)	Broad dome	Russet	Fine timber
Turkey oak (Q cerris)	Tall dome, open crown		Great vigour, poor timber
Beech (Fagus sylvatica)	Tall dome, broad	Orange-brown	Unsafe when old. Bears a little shade. Good timber.
Sweet chestnut (Castanea sativa)	Tall dome, broad with great age	Yellow, russet	Great vigour, long-lived. Good timber but often split and shaken.
Small-leafed lime (Tilia cordata)	Big dome, dense		Usually vigorous. Attractive foliage. Soft white timber.
Large-leafed lime (T platyphyllos)	Broad dome		Vigorous, good shape
Ash (Fraxinus excelsior)	High, open dome		Fast on rich, damp soil, when timber of high quality. Roots rob soil when near crops.
Grey poplar (Populus canescens)	High dome	Yellow	Silvery foliage in spring. Vigorous. Strong roots and suckers.
Sycamore (Acer pseudo-platanus)	Broad, dense dome		Damaged by squirrels. Unpopular with farmers and conservationists. Timber good.
Hornbeam (Carpinus betulus)	Broad, fine twigs	Light russet	Attractive. Quite vigorous. Timber too hard for normal use, very strong.
White willow (Salix alba)	Tall, acute, then domed		Vigorous. Pale blue-grey.
Italian alder (Alnus cordata)	Tall, conic, dense		Vigorous, adaptable and handsome
Norway maple (Acer platanoides)	Broad dome	Gold, orange or red	Mass of yellow flowers in April. Vigorous. continued

II. Medium stature

Common alder (Alnus glutinosa)	Conic		Base-rich, very moist soils preferred
Crack willow (Salix fragilis)	Broad, low dome	Brief yellow	Long, glossy, bright leaves. Handsome.
Grey alder (Alnus incana)	Broad column		Vigorous on wide variety of soils
Gean or wild cherry (Prunus avium)	Broad dome	Yellow, pink and dark red	Mass of white flowers in early May. High quality timber.
Bird cherry (P padus)	Ovoid	Yellow, pink	Tassels of white flowers in June
Field maple (Acer campestre)	Broad, dense dome	Gold, some crimson	Exceptionally, up to 80' tall. Fairly fast growing.
Wild service tree (Sorbus torminalis)	Conic, then domed	Crimson, dark red	Very handsome, unusual native.

Hedges near Orchards

Hedges can be used to protect orchard and other fruit crops from storm and frost. Care must be taken with siting and management. Shelter planting cannot be covered in detail here but a few indications of requirements are in order.

HEDGE AND ORCHARD DISEASES

Coral spot, apple mildews, silver leaf and honey fungus can all spread from host trees into an orchard. Silver leaf is particularly associated with poplars, so these should be avoided as screen plants near plums. Where raspberries and blackberries are cultivated their wild relatives should be kept out of the hedgerow since they may carry the virus diseases mosaic and dwarfing. Pine trees having five needles, such as Weymouth pine, should not be planted as screens near blackcurrants since they are alternate hosts of blackcurrant rust disease (Beddall, 1950, p 59). For comments on fireblight, a particularly serious disease, see page 20.

SITING THE ORCHARD HEDGE

a   The hedge should be at least 25 yards (23m) from the first row of fruit trees so that the hedge roots will not rob the soil in the orchard.

b   Hedges should be sited so as to protect the fruit from wind frost, which can ruin an otherwise 'frost free' hillside orchard. Wind frost occurs when moving air is below 32°F (0°C). The most damage occurs in the spring, during blossom time, because the delicate organs of the flowers are damaged when the flower temperature falls below 29°F (-1.5°C) for half an hour or more. Fruitlets are damaged just below the freezing point while unopened flowers can withstand 5° or 6°F (about 3°C) of frost unharmed.

c   Hedges should be sited to help prevent radiation frost. Radiation frost, which is more common than wind frost, occurs on still clear nights when surfaces cool rapidly. Cold air is unable to hold much moisture and so deposits it as dew on cold surface objects. If the surface is below freezing point the moisture forms as hoar frost. Even in May severe radiation frosts can occur when the temperature of the grass may fall to 20°F (-7°C).

Cooling air sinks and flows downhill. The danger is that it will collect in pockets and valleys, building up until it surrounds the fruit trees, frosting them. Hedges planted across the top of an orchard can divert frosty air to one side. The hedge should be placed oblique to the slope, not directly across it where it may act as a dam blocking the cold air until it spills over.

d   Hedges must never be placed where they will augment radiation frosts. A dense hedge at the low end of an orchard will block cold air from flowing away downhill. This air can build up until it envelopes the fruit trees. For example, a layer of cold air only 2" (50mm) deep, gathered from 200 acres (80 hectares) of hillside and confined within a 4 acre (1.6 hectare) orchard will build up to 8'-9' (2.4m-2.7m) deep.

To prevent this, a gap must be left in the hedge at its lowest point in order for the air to drain through. The size of the gap depends on the size of the area from which cold air collects and on the contours of the land. In the example given above, a 20' (6m) gap would be sufficient, but if the hedge were a long one several gaps would be needed.

To form a gap for cold air outflow, cut the side branches off the stems of the hedge trees to a height of 3'-4' (1m) above the ground. Always keep the grass cut down around the stems so it will not block the air flow.

e   Even if radiation frost were not a danger, orchard hedges should allow a flow-through of air because scab diseases on apples and pears can spread in moist, stagnant air.

ESTABLISHING AND MANAGING THE ORCHARD HEDGE

a   The hedge must be 10'-12' (3m-3.7m) tall to provide adequate wind shelter.

b   A shelter hedge should be three or four rows deep, preferably in an arc shape with the convex side towards the wind.

c   If the site is exposed, plant the hedge with young specimens. They become established more quickly under stress than do older ones.

The most common trees for windbreaks are Leyland cypress (X <u>Cupressocyparis</u> <u>leylandii</u>), grey alder (<u>Alnus</u> <u>incana</u>) and the poplar <u>Populus</u> <u>hybrid</u> 32. Other suitable trees include larch, spruce, Scots pine, Austrian pine, western red cedar (<u>Thuja</u> <u>plicata</u>) and beech (if space allows). For further information on windbreaks see MAFF (1968).

d   Plant shelter hedge trees at 6' (1.8m) intervals. As the trees reach maturity thin the hedge by removing alternate trees. Quick growers, such as poplars, can be used as nurse trees for slower-growing trees such as spruce or pine and can be cut out completely when the others become tall enough.

e   Small standard trees such as damsons can be planted in the hedgerow for wind protection, allowing the hedge to remain a reasonable size.

f   Keep all rubbish out of the hedge bottom. Make sure that grass is mown and branches lopped where necessary to form cold air gaps.

6 Trimming

Trimming, also known as 'paring', 'brushing', 'breasting', or 'switching', is an annual event for most farm and estate hedges. Trimming usually means short-back-and-sides, the hedge frequently cut to a squat square profile. This is the simplest form to cut but not the best one for hedge growth nor for wildlife.

Some farmers try to trim indefinitely, not realising that it is almost impossible to preserve a stockproof hedge in this way. A few farmers do not trim at all but simply let the hedge grow until it is ready for laying. In most cases a balance is needed, depending on how the land manager evaluates the relative arguments for and against trimming and laying.

Trimming versus Laying

The following points summarise the pros and cons of each form of management.

TRIMMING

a   The cost is low but must be borne each year. If you lack the necessary machine you must hire a contractor and the cost becomes much higher.

b   The vigour and stockproof qualities of the hedge are gradually reduced by regular trimming over a number of years, and can only be restored by occasional laying (see below).

c   In some hedges the shrubs were originally spaced too widely for trimming. They were designed to be cut and laid often, the pleachers bridging the gaps between plants. Some species, particularly hawthorn, send out lateral shoots into these gaps when top cut. Others, such as hazel and field maple, respond to trimming by sending up new straight shoots from the stools. These will never fill gaps between plants, so trimming alone cannot maintain the stockproof qualities of this type of hedge.

d   Prolonged management by trimming may substantially increase the difficulty and therefore the cost of eventual laying.

e   The entire hedge is disturbed each year. Work is usually done in summer or autumn, when damage to wildlife can be considerable. Nesting birds in particular are harmed if work is done before midsummer. Late winter trimming, after most of the berries have been eaten by birds, allows them better use of the hedge but destroys certain overwintering insects and reduces next spring's flowering.

The quality of the habitat after disturbance depends to some extent upon the shape to which the hedge is trimmed (see below) but the value of the hedge for birds and invertebrates remains poor compared to the untrimmed, well-grown but stockproof hedge.

It may be that the composition of plant species in the hedge is affected over many years of trimming due to the better response of some shrubs than others to this management. Further studies are needed on this question.

f   Additional periodic work is necessary to check the hedge for elder and climbing plants. These must be grubbed up if they are not to eventually choke out preferred species and ruin the hedge's stockproof quality.

g   If trimming is done mechanically it may be difficult to notice and leave promising saplings to develop into hedgerow trees. This is particularly the case with the less flexible machines such as the flail and the shapesaw (p 65).

CUTTING AND LAYING

a   The cost is very high but is borne only every eight to twenty years or in some situations even less frequently.

b   A skilled hedge layer may be difficult to find.

c   With regular laying the hedge remains vigorous and stockproof indefinitely, possibly for centuries.

d   Normally only a portion of the hedge system is disturbed in any one year. This disturbance is very great, but it comes when the direct effects are likely to be least harmful unless work is done late in the season in early spring.

The value of the newly laid hedge for birds is poor. But within three or four years it surpasses that of the trimmed hedge and continues to improve until it is again cut and laid. As it nears full size, however, it may attract crows, rooks and pigeons at cost to other wildlife and to farmers.

e   Elder and climbing plants are normally grubbed up or cut out of the hedge during laying. There is little likelihood that they will choke out preferred shrubs. Laying appears to favour the thorns against most other species.

f   It is easy to select and leave saplings to develop into hedgerow trees.

Trimming and Laying

Most landowners who want permanently stockproof hedges trim each year but lay occasionally whenever a hedge begins to go thin at the base. This rotation may be cheaper than more frequent laying with no trimming and allows control over the hedge's shape and size during most years. Managers can plan to lay the hedge when most convenient since it seldom matters, within a margin of a few years, when this is done.

A few farmers, particularly in the Midlands, prefer not to trim their hedges at all. They feel that trimming hardly allows enough postponement of laying to be worth the bother. Also, even if the hedge is allowed to 'lie fallow' between trimming and laying, it is never as straight and clean after it has been trimmed. Where hedges grow quickly and must in any case be laid fairly frequently, it may be worth keeping the hedge in the best possible shape for easiest and quickest laying.

Two precautions are necessary to successfully integrate annual trimming with occasional laying:

a   The hedge must be brought into condition for laying. It does no good to miss out one summer's trim and expect to lay it that winter. The stems will be far too short to make adequate pleachers and they will be twisted and interlocked, making work difficult. The hedge must be left alone for two to five years, depending on how fast it grows and on how much of a rat's nest the branches are in. Where they are very twisted and gnarled due to prolonged trimming it is well worth leaving the hedge for the longer period. New straight shoots will grow up; by the end of the 'fallow' time the twisted growth will have died because it can't compete; when you come to lay the hedge you will find that much of the apparent tangle breaks up with no struggle.

b   After the hedge is laid it should again be left 'fallow' in order to develop strength and thickness in the new growth to allow it to withstand trimming. Trimming can resume after one or two growing seasons.

The Effects of Trimming

Trimming seems to accelerate and exaggerate the ageing of the shrubs. An initially stockproof hedge, if trimmed each year but never cut and laid, eventually goes through the progression outlined below. Hedges managed for trimming from the time they are planted never require heavy top-cutting and so keep healthier longer, with less distortion of their form, than mature hedges which are topped and lopped to be forced into shape.

1   Shoots proliferate from just below the cut ends of the stems. There is some increase in side branching. Each shrub species responds slightly differently to trimming. In general, though, the effect is as diagrammed:

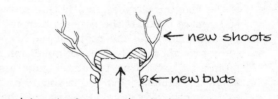

cut heals from outside to centre

The stems continue to thicken each year just as in normal trees. The cut surfaces develop into knobs of scar tissue as the cuts heal over.

2   The first stage continues, leading among lateral-branching shrubs such as hawthorn to increasingly deformed and interlocked branches. This happens gradually over several years, with a result similar to the natural stunting that occurs where hedges grow in harsh climatic conditions.

During stages one and two the hedge remains stockproof and may become even stronger due to the increasingly dense outer growth and the interlocking of each plant's branches with those of its neighbours.

3   Eventually, the bottom and inner branches die back. This leads to the development of gaps at the base of the hedge and a shell-like growth form.

This may occur after ten or twelve annual trims or, in exceptional cases, not for half a century. Under normal conditions about twenty years is average before gapping becomes serious. Even thorns, most robust of the hedging shrubs, finally thin at the base and centre because the dense outer and upper growth shades out the rest. If the hedge is to be brought back to perfect condition for laying it must not be trimmed once this stage is reached. Instead it should be left to grow away for several years until suitable for laying.

Sometime during this stage the hedge ceases to be sheep proof.

4   The hedge gradually loses vigour, signalled by slow regrowth after trimming and the beginning of die-back in weaker plants. Every year trimmed plants must put energy into late-season growth to make up for the loss of their spring production. They cannot store energy as the summer goes on and so lose strength.

5   The main stems continue to thicken but there are now only a few very gnarled side branches. Foliage is confined increasingly to the top of the hedge. Shoots which have been cut repeatedly at about the same level are unable to put up new growth through the mass of dead stems and scar tissue, so twigs and smaller branches die. Die-back progresses in towards the main stems and, as they break up, the adjacent plants lose their 'grip' on each other leading to the formation of gaps. Gaps may become extensive as weak plants

die completely.

If the hedge has not been breached by cattle already it will be now. But still it can be revived, if die-back has not gone too far. Many farmers let their hedges get to this stage before leaving them alone to grow up for laying. The important thing is to stop trimming before the plants lose their ability to send up straight strong shoots.

6   The hedge is dying or derelict, more gap than barrier, although surviving shrubs may spread into the air space left by neighbours if the dead plants are cut out. Some species, notably blackthorn and elm, sucker readily into these gaps, but in other cases only occasional half-alive stubs remain.

The hedge is probably too far gone for laying even if it is now left alone. However renovation may still be possible, although with difficulty (p 70).

Work Season

Traditionally, trimming took place twice a year, first in early spring before the sap rose and again in the autumn after most growth had stopped. These days costs and labour shortage usually reduce trimming to one cut per year. This can be done at any time other than May or June, the height of the growing season. Trimming at this time allows too much second growth and unnecessarily saps the hedge's strength.

From a wildlife viewpoint trimming should be avoided in spring, summer and autumn. Trimming before August disturbs nesting birds, while trimming in either summer or autumn cuts off the developing buds and berries which are winter food for many animals. Therefore, when possible, trimming should be held off until late winter when most of this food has been utilised. Late trimming, though, allows much more shrub growth the next season and so results in a taller bushier hedge.

Avoid major cutting and lopping during hard frosts since the cambium may freeze, damaging the shrubs, and since many species are brittle under these conditions.

Profile and Height

HEDGE PROFILES

Rectangular   A-shaped   Chamfered   Topped A   Rounded

The diagram indicates the basic profiles to which hedges can be trimmed. The height can be varied relative to the width to produce any number of final shapes.

The choice of profile and height depends on several factors:

a   Stock fencing requirements. The only limitation here is that the hedge be high enough and that long-term growth be enhanced as much as possible. A 3' (910mm) to 3'6" (1060mm) hedge is adequate for sheep (breeds differ in their hedge-running abilities), but 4' (1220mm) to 4'6" (1370mm) is required for cattle. The A-shape, because it tapers to the top, must be left taller than the other forms to keep it cattleproof.

b   Shelter or windbreak requirements. The general effect of hedges on wind are examined on pages 17-18. Two points should be added here. The A-shaped or topped A hedge makes the most effective windbreak because it allows wind to pass over it with less turbulence than the flat-fronted shape. In arable fields a tall hedge, over say 6' (1.8m), may if very dense be of less value than a lower hedge because it causes wind turbulence behind the hedge which lays the corn there.

EFFECTS OF HEDGE SHAPE ON WIND (section)

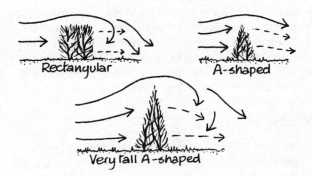

c   Effects on long-term growth. Hedgers express conflicting opinions based on their experiences with local conditions. Some say the rectangular hedge regrows best because

a large top area is exposed to sunlight. Most hedgers argue the opposite, that regrowth is comparatively poor because at least one side is likely to be severely shaded. In addition, the tight, dense top inhibits growth in the centre. A third disadvantage is that heavy snowfall can accumulate on the flat top and crush and distort the hedge.

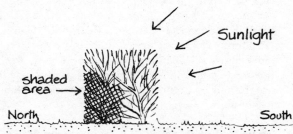

SELF SHADING OF RECTANGULAR HEDGE

The A-shaped hedge exposes both surfaces to maximum sunlight while allowing snowfall to slip off. Regrowth is best if the more shaded side is trimmed to a more gradual batter, allowing low branches to get as much light as possible. Rectangular hedges which show signs of gapping on the shady side can sometimes be brought back to good condition by trimming to the A-shape. But against the A-shape is the argument that trimming 'nibbles the shoots' on the near or ditch side of the Midlands type hedge, due to its asymmetrical cross-section. This is shown in the diagram on the next page.

Chamfered, topped A and rounded designs try in different ways to combat the problems of the two more common styles. The chamfered shape increases the height at which shoots are cut on the Midlands type hedge while preserving some of the light-catching and snow-slipping qualities of the A-shape. The topped A is suitable for a symmetrical hedge where it is believed that top growth is stimulated by being cut flat. The rounded form provides the greatest strength against snow since it is streamlined yet is not as vulnerably thin at the top as the A-shaped hedge.

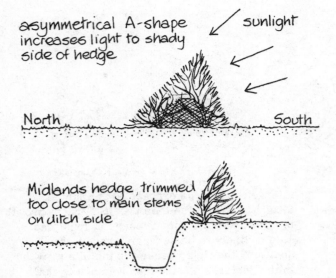

asymmetrical A-shape increases light to shady side of hedge

sunlight

North   South

Midlands hedge, trimmed too close to main stems on ditch side

d   Effects on wildlife. The only effect of trimming which has been much investigated is that of height on nesting bird success. The too-common yard-high hedge subjects nesting birds to ground predators. Hedges of 4'-5' (1220mm-1520mm) provide some protection but hedges 6' (1830mm) or higher are by far the most suitable. Practically speaking, this height can be achieved only by cutting to the A-shape.

e   Technical problems. Here the arguments have to do with the sort of machine used and the number of passes required to trim to each shape. Many machines have a cutting surface of only 3' (910mm) which is why so many hedges are trimmed to one yard square in profile. Although the A-shape hedge has but two surfaces to cut, few machines can do them at a single pass on each side so the time required for clipping is likely to be greater than for the rectangular or topped A hedge. The chamfered design has five surfaces, each requiring a pass of the machine. However this may be no more time-consuming to cut than a relatively tall three-surfaced hedge whose sides need two passes each. The rounded form is suited to hand or hand-held power trimming rather than large machines. By hand methods it seems neither easier nor harder than the other profiles.

Machine Trimming

The past quarter century has seen the disappearance of the craftsman trimmer and now nearly all farm hedges are trimmed mechanically with tractor-mounted cutters. Most disadvantages of machine trimming can be overcome if the right machine is used, the cutter kept properly maintained and

sharp, and work not attempted when fields are extremely soft.

ADVANTAGE

a   Machine trimming is quick and comparatively cheap. Estimates in 1984 were about £9-10 per hour for flail cutting of annual growth. The length of hedge cut in an hour would depend on ground conditions, hedge height, width and shape, but 700 – 1,000 yards should be managed with no trouble. Estimates for cutting larger growth using a shapesaw were £13-15 per hour, the length of hedge cut being dependent on its condition.

DISADVANTAGES

a   Machine trimming may be very ragged, particularly when a flail is used on large, overgrown shrubs. This is visually distressing and may leave the hedge more open to fungus infection.

b   Machine trimming is noisy and disturbing. However, other farm tasks are equally so.

c   Machines cannot always get where needed at the right time. If taken through very wet fields they may compact and harm the soil. They cannot reach hedges on inaccessible steep slopes or those with awkward corners.

d   Certain obstacles are difficult to work around. Telephone poles, trees, etc alongside the hedge interfere with and slow down the work.

TYPES OF MECHANICAL HEDGE TRIMMERS

Different types of tractor-mounted trimmers and cutters are designed for rather different uses. Anyone contemplating buying such equipment should carefully consider his budget and requirements and the compatibility of his tractor with various makes and models of trimmers. Full coverage is not possible here, but the three main types of mechanical trimmer are described below.

Cutter-bar

The reciprocating cutter-bar does by far the neatest job of the three types of trimmers but is suitable only for hedges in good condition since it cannot cut thick stems. It is easier and cheaper to maintain, and faster for annual trims, than circular saws.

Flail

The flail mower is a general purpose chopping, chewing and mulching tool that can be used not only on hedges but for clearing small shrubs and rough herbage on ditch and dyke sides, banks and headlands. It does a surprisingly neat job on light or medium growth but is often used for the heavy work of lopping overgrown hedges where it is much less efficient than a shape saw and leaves a ragged, shattered remnant.

This is the most commonly used hedging and mowing machine, and many types are available. In general though, they can be divided into light flails, which cut branches up to 1" (25mm) thick, and heavy flails, which cut branches up to 4" (100mm) thick.

Shapesaw

The shapesaw is designed for lopping overgrown hedges or for cutting them near to ground level for regrowth from the base. On big jobs the most economical method is to go around the hedge with a flail to take off the sides and mulch them up and then change to a saw attachment to cut down the main stems for burning. Shapesaws come with either circular saw blades for cutting up to 8" (200mm) growth or 'slasher' or 'scimitar' blades for lighter material up to 3" (75mm) diameter. Saw blades are most costly to maintain since they need to be sharpened and set by a saw doctor, while the slasher and scimitar blades can be maintained by the user. Stems thicker than 8" should be removed first with a power saw.

The following manufacturers can supply various types of hedging machinery:

R. S. Fleming Developments, 1 Cosgrove Road, Old Stratford, Milton Keynes MK19 6AG, supply Fleming Power Heads, which are shapesaws that fit most types of hydraulic powered flail hedgecutters.

Turner International (Engineering) Ltd, Kings Coughton, Alcester, Warwickshire have a comprehensive range of flail cutters, a 36" (900mm) circular saw and ditch cleaning bucket.

Hydrocut Ltd, Sudbury, Suffolk manufacture a multi-purpose flail head, with a knife/chisel flail combination for cutting anything from grass up to medium size hedge growth. They also supply a 10' (3m) long cutter bar, which can reach up to 30' (9m) high, and is used particularly on shelter hedges around orchards, hop fields and so on. Hydrocut Ltd also supply rough cut, slasher and saw blades.

When cutting with a cutter bar or shapesaw, the order of cutting should be firstly hedgebank, then side and finally top, to allow the cuttings to fall clear of the hedge, and ease the job of clearing up. The reverse order should be followed when using a flail cutter, as this allows the flails to progressively pulverise the cuttings.

Common faults resulting from poor mechanical hedge cutting are:

a   'Buck headed' hedges. This occurs where frequent light trimmings, each further out from the centre of the hedge that the last, results in a tall 'leggy' hedge which is thin and gappy at the base. This should be cut back hard with a flail or shape saw to encourage new growth at the base.

b   Undercut hedges. This is the result of verge or bank cutting being done too close to the centre of the hedge, so weakening the hedge at its most important part for stock control, which is the bottom 2' (600mm).

c   Very small hedges. Over enthusiastic tidying can reduce a hedge until it is so small as to be virtually useless.

The A-shaped or topped A-shaped hedge described above has several advantages for mechanical cutting operations.

a   Cuttings fall off, and not into the hedge.

b   In some cases, fewer passes of the machine are required than when cutting a square-topped hedge.

c   There is less danger to the tractor driver in using a flail head or shapesaw on an A-shape, as debris is directed downwards, and not towards the tractor cab.

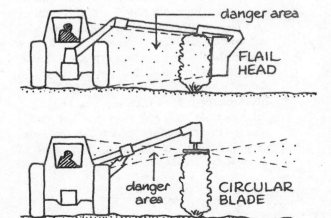

d   Saplings can easily be left at the apex of the
     A-shape, to grow into hedgerow trees.

e   Growth is encouraged lower down at the base
     of the hedge, where it is most needed.

Safety

Used carelessly or without prior training, these
mechanical hedge trimmers can be extremely
dangerous. The Agricultural Training Board
produce a series of detailed trainee guides in the
maintenance and safe use of tractor mounted
hedge trimmers. Three other booklets, from
which some of the above information is taken,
deal with special considerations and advice on
the cutting of neglected, well-maintained or new
hedges with this equipment. The booklets (codes
LBM 2.B.1 - 2.B.7) are available from the ATB
Training Centre, National Agricultural Centre,
Kenilworth, Warwickshire CV8 2LG.

Hand Trimming

ADVANTAGES

a   Close inspection of the hedge is possible
     while working. Promising saplings can be
     left to develop into hedgerow trees if these
     are wanted. Vines and climbers can be cut
     out; elder can be cut at ground level or,
     preferably, grubbed up.

b   Disturbance while working can be minimised.
     Hand trimming with billhook and slasher,
     although not with powered tools, is quiet
     and leisurely; wild animals have time to
     get away. The trimmed hedge is just as
     changed as when machine cut, but the
     field is less disturbed and the soil is not
     compacted.

c   Work can be done when and where machine
     access is impracticable. Hand trimming
     is possible at any season, though it should
     not be done in May or June for the sake of
     hedge shrubs and nesting birds. Winter,
     when machines must be kept off most
     fields, is best for minimum wildlife
     disturbance. Few farm hedges are
     inaccessible to large machines but else-
     where tractor access may be impossible
     or unjustifiable in terms of the amount of
     work to be done.

DISADVANTAGE

Hand trimming is labour-intensive and many times
costlier than machine work where machines are
available and have access to a site.

TOOLS

Hand-held power tools

Some early farm hedge trimming machines were
designed to be hand-held and to run off portable
motors or tractor generators. These days, most
available hand-held trimmers are designed for
the estate and garden market where a neat job
rather than speed or ability to handle thick stems
is important. Wolf Tools for Garden and Lawn
Ltd, Ross-on-Wye, Herefordshire supply electric
reciprocating trimmers with 21" (530mm) blades
and a 13½" (340mm) cordless rechargeable
battery model, suitable for light work.

Larger trimmers, designed to professional
standards, are available from Birds Grass-Care,
Crossways, Cowbridge, South Glamorgan CF7 7LJ.
These include the Allen Hedgecutter HF108, which
has a 22.6cc engine and 31" (800mm) blade, and
the Allen Trucut 16 with a 16" (400mm) blade.
Also available are the Mountfield MT100, with
16cc engine and 24" (600mm) blade, and the
Mountfield MT240, with 23cc engine and 30"
(760mm) blade.

Black and Decker, Cannon Lane, Maidenhead,
Berkshire SL6 3PD, manufacture a range of
electric hedging clippers with 12" (300mm),
16" (400mm) or 24" (600mm) blades, designed
for garden use.

Billhooks and slashers

The two tools generally used for hand trimming
farm hedges are billhook and slasher. Where
the hedge is fairly short and has been kept in
regular trim the billhook usually does the
cleaner job. The slasher, however, gives a
larger sweep per stroke and with it you can reach
up or down without extra effort. Shears may be
used but, while producing a neat finish, they are
very slow to use.

Traditionally there were various specialised forms
of bills and slashers designed for hedge trimming,
but most of these are now unavailable. A common
tool was the single-edged billhook blade on the
end of a slasher handle. The 'switching bill'
was a lightweight (2lb) shorthandled billhook with
a 7"-8" x 2½" blade, again with a single edge.
A few antiques are illustrated opposite.

Whatever the available range of bills and slashers, the best for trimming hedges in the opinion of most craftsmen today are those which combine lightness and a straight cutting edge. Annual trimming is fairly light work, unlike the trimming that is done prior to laying the hedge.

There is no need for the hook or weighted nose of some bills or the curved blade of some slashers.

Herefordshire hedge trimming bills
~ early 19ᵗʰ Century
(after Beddall, 1950, p 33)
All used with long handles

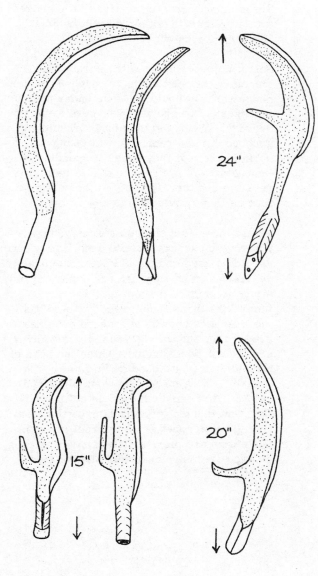

24"

15"

20"

TECHNIQUE

Keep in mind the following points:

a Tools must be very sharp. Otherwise the job will take longer, be more dangerous and probably result in a poor finish. A splintered and battered hand-trimmed hedge is just as liable to fungus attack as one massacred by machine.

b Most hedgers recommend cutting with an upward stroke of slasher or billhook where possible. This produces a clean cut, less likely to fray and peel back the bark than if you cut down. Some hedgers recommend the oblique upward cut for restoring a hedge which has not been regularly trimmed, but an oblique downward cut for a hedge which is already correctly shaped through previous annual trimmings. The idea is that, done regularly, downward cutting encourages downward growth and within two or three years produces a thick resilient stockproof skirt around the sides of the hedge.

c Trim in towards a gap from either side to help new growth come in and close it.

7 Preliminaries to Hedge Laying

This chapter covers preliminary considerations before laying a hedge. Technical and procedural notes are contained in the following two chapters.

Where a hedge serves as a stock fence it should be periodically renewed by cutting and laying. In this process the living stems or 'pleachers' are cut part way through at the base and then bent over at an angle. The pleachers form an effective barrier for a number of years, until eventually they die back and rot away. By the time this has happened new shoots have sprung from the cut stools of the pleachers to form a strong, vigorous replacement 'crop' of stems. Thus laying keeps the hedge youthful indefinitely.

As single plants age they finally stop responding to treatment. How long they last depends on the type of shrub, the climate and soil and the maintenance programme. When they start to die they should be grubbed out and replaced (p 52).

Frequency of Laying

It is more important to be able to judge when a hedge has reached the right stage for laying than it is to know when it was last laid. In good conditions, as on a fairly heavy but reasonably drained soil in sheltered situations, thorn hedges may have to be laid every seven to ten years if they are not top cut in between. The average interval between laying for untrimmed hedges is fifteen to twenty years, but in uplands or whenever conditions are harsh the hedge will grow more slowly and thirty years or more may pass before the hedge is ready to be laid again. Hedges managed by annual trimming may continue for half a century before the bottom starts to thin out showing that the hedge should be allowed to grow up for laying. This is exceptional; more often trimming only slightly extends the intervals between laying. Different tree species respond differently to cutting and laying and regrow at different speeds, influenced of course by climate, soil and management. Growth and survival characteristics for some shrubs are included in the chapter, 'Planting and Early Care'.

Optimum State of Hedge for Laying

a   For the management of a new hedge prior to first laying, see pages 53-4.

b   Stems to be used as pleachers should be 8'-12' (2.4m-3.6m) tall. If they are much shorter or taller than this it will be hard to make a good hedge from them although with care a wide range of lengths can be used for pleachers.

If the hedge has been managed by top cutting it should be left to grow up for three to four years before laying.

c   Stems for pleachers should be sturdy but not so thick that they are hard to cut and lay. Ideally they should be about 2"-4" (50mm - 100mm) in diameter at the base. Very thin pleachers add little to the strength of the hedge but are often laid in anyway to increase its density and to encourage more growth from the base of these stems. Very thick pleachers are difficult to lay without breaking and hard to position in the hedge without displacing other pleachers or knocking stakes out of line.

d   Select vigorous and healthy shrubs for pleaching. Once they have reached maturity hedge shrubs should continue under proper management to provide pleachers for many decades. Weak and old shrubs should be grubbed out and replaced with young nursery trees if they cease responding to management. In practice this is seldom possible and they are kept in the hedge as long as they provide some new growth.

Where there is a choice between young vigorous pleachers and old ones, the young should be used and the old cut at the base to resprout as best they can. The bark of old stems is gnarled and corky. Thorn's inner bark turns from greenish to red as the tree ages and the heartwood becomes greyer than that of vigorous stems which are a clean white inside. Often the base of the old tree is attacked by fungus or 'canker' which makes the wood black and pulpy. This canker should be cut away if the stem is used for pleaching or the stem should be pleached from the root (p 83). Old stems are more brittle than young ones and require more care when laying (see point c, p 71).

Auxiliary Work

Hedge laying often involves additional work which must be planned in advance.

a   Collection or burning of cuttings and collection of unburnable rubbish. This involves additional time or manpower and the co-operation of the land owner or manager, especially if a tractor and trailer is needed to cart away the remains. Be completely sure of your clean-up responsibilities before beginning work to avoid misunderstandings and wasted effort later.

b   Clearance of the ditch or repair and turfing of the bank. Most hedges have one or both of these features. Traditionally ditches and banks were maintained at the same time as the hedge was laid, although not necessarily by the same worker. Although they require additional tools these tasks can be integrated into group hedge laying for efficiency. Ditching is carried out after the hedge has been laid; banking and turfing before the hedge has been laid but after the preliminary cleaning out has been finished. See page 76 for a brief treatment of ditching. Banking and turfing are discussed in a chapter on their own.

c   Protection of the hedge after laying. This is discussed below.

Protecting the Newly Laid Hedge

The protection needed depends on the type of hedge and the use planned for the adjacent land over the next year or two, ie until new growth gets fairly started, and to a lesser extent thereafter. Climate may also be a factor. In all cases the aim is to ensure that new shoots develop unhindered until they are unpalatable and tough enough to discourage browsing by animals.

If neither side of the hedge is subject to grazing, no measures need be taken unless snow is a problem (see below). Midlands hedges need no protection against livestock on the field side, as long as the original hedge is satisfactorily thick and the workmanship good, but the near or ditch side must be kept free from grazing. As one craftsman put it, ' lambs and beasts will get to chittering at the new shoots and stunt the growth' unless temporary barbed wire fencing is strung along the ditch, on the side away from the hedge, or unless stock is kept off the field for a year or

two. Thorn cuttings piled into the ditch discourage animals but do not guarantee immunity to grazing.

Banked hedges vary considerably in their need for protection. Unless they are also ditched they are seldom cattle-proof, and even where the bank is high enough to protect the living hedge from grazing the bank itself may be damaged. In the days of labour-intensive husbandry, a fair bit of the herdsman's time was probably taken up with preventing his beasts' too-thorough investigation of the hedge. These days it is best to put up a permanent fence (p 52). Although it may seem to defeat the purpose of the hedge, in fact the combination of hedge and simple fence is probably cheapest in the long run unless you are in a position to check your hedge very frequently and repair the bank and fill in small gaps as they appear. Even so a fence is required for the first couple of growing seasons after the hedge is laid.

Welsh hedges, in general, are designed to be firm against sheep and various stratagems are used to protect the shoots. In some cases, as with the high-banked Flying Hedge or the thick, wide Double Brush, the hedge itself protects the new shoots on both sides. In central Wales thinner hedges are sometimes guarded by piles of brushwood trimmings placed along the sides of the bank and up to the edges of the cut hedge. A Montgomeryshire variation of this technique is the use of 'byrdn', small dead cuttings placed neatly and deliberately along the top of the newly-turfed bank. The byrdn is put in after the turfing is completed but before the pleachers are cut and laid. As you cut the unwanted growth out of the hedge, take brushy ends and cut each so that when stuck into the bank they are half as high as the eventual height of the laid hedge. Sharpen the base of each stem with the billhook and force it into the comb of the bank, angled just as the pleachers will be, along and slightly outward from the bank. (See diagram next page).

Brushwood also protects the hedge in those exceptional circumstances where it is subject to heavy winter snowdrift. This is only likely where it runs across a slope with the prevailing storm winds coming down the hill toward it. In this case the weight of snow can distort the hedge, push the pleachers apart and crush the new shoots. The brushwood should be placed along the side where drifts build up, staked every few yards to help keep it in position.

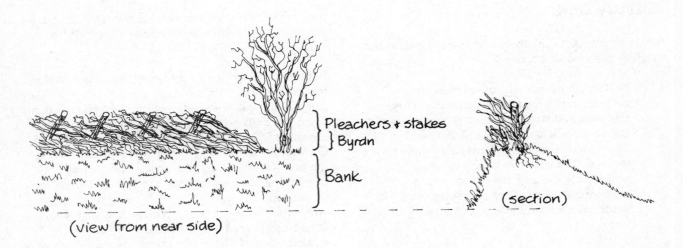

Pleachers + stakes
} Byrdn

Bank

(view from near side)

(section)

Restoring the Neglected Hedge

Where it is not thought necessary to restore the
hedge to a condition for laying, but it is to be
kept as a shelter belt or for amenity purposes,
it should be cleaned up to occupy as narrow a
line as possible where adjacent land uses have
priority (eg agricultural land or footpaths). A
permanent fence must be erected along the
entire length if a stockproof barrier is needed.
The fence should be put up well clear of the
hedge.

Where the aim is to re-establish the hedge to a
condition suitable for laying and normal
maintenance, remedial action can take one of
three forms depending on the state of the hedge.
'Ribbing' or 'siding back', for the overgrown
hedge with few gaps, is outlined by LeSueur
(1951, p71). The other two methods are
described by the Ministry of Agriculture,
Fisheries and Food (1982, p 10). In every case
the bank or ditch should be repaired as needed
and a temporary fence erected against grazing
until the hedge has regrown. Rabbit fencing
may be necessary for new plantings (p 52).

'RIBBING'' OR ''SIDING BACK'

This is the simplest solution where the hedge is
wide and spreading but has few gaps. However
it does not necessarily produce the best hedge
for laying. The work should be done in March
or April if the situation is exposed, or otherwise
any time during the winter except in frosty
weather. There are two methods. In both
cases the trimming aims to produce a sloping,
A-form hedge.

a   Top the hedge and then cut to within 6''
(150mm) of the main stems on each side.
Since this is a strain on the plants it is

best to do one side one year and the other
side the next, or better, two years later.
Since the plants are cut rather high they will
tend to go bare at the base and be difficult
to lay in the future if this method is used.

b   Where the hedge is in a double row and the
stems are healthy and not too large, cut
one side to the stump and leave the other
untouched or only slightly trimmed until the
cut side has regrown. This method is best
for thick regrowth from ground level.
However it is more dangerous for the hedge
since the uncut side may shade out the cut
side.

LAYING, REPLANTING AND FENCING THE GAPS

Where there are moderate gaps and suitable
pleachers, lay pleachers into the gaps and peg
them down to root (p 85). Where this is not
possible but in general the hedge is ready for
laying it can be laid, new plants put into the gaps
and the gaps fenced. Otherwise the gaps can be
planted first and laying postponed until the new
plants have grown tall enough. See 'Planting up
gaps' (p 52).

If the hedge is trimmed between layings, trim
towards the gap from both sides to encourage
growth over the gap (p 67).

CUTTING DOWN AND FENCING FOR REGROWTH

Coppicing is a common form of management for
certain hedges. However, coppicing takes place
at fairly short intervals, usually ten to fifteen
years, whereas in this case the hedge is assumed
to be old, large and sprawling. Since cutting to
the ground is harder on the shrubs than laying,

this treatment should only be undertaken when laying is not practicable or when the stockproof qualities of the hedge are not paramount. Hawthorn usually resprouts well after this treatment unless it is very old, as does field maple. Other species, though, are often killed by it.

Remember these points:

a   Cut off the stems an inch or two above ground level. Do not cut them higher if you want the hedge to regenerate properly: the plants will bush out at the tops of the cut stems but the bases will remain as bare as ever and later cutting and laying will be nearly impossible.

b   Cut out and, preferably, grub up any old and decaying stumps.

c   New growth from the cut stems will be strongly upright. Therefore gaps between stems will not close themselves. Large gaps should be replanted and small gaps pleached over when the hedge is next laid.

Work Season and Weather Precautions

a   Hedge laying is generally done between late September/early October and late March/early May. The time varies somewhat with the local climate. The sap should have gone from the leaves before work begins although the leaves may not have fallen. It is best to stop when the buds have burst in the spring. The only time which must be avoided is the season of vigorous new growth.

In southern England and the Midlands hedge laying continues throughout the winter. In upland areas including most of Wales it is considered best to lay before Christmas or again after about mid-February to avoid the risk of hard frosts. But this depends very much on local conditions; some places in cold parts of the country remain frost-free while otherwise mild areas may contain frost pockets in certain spots.

b   Avoid laying a hedge during or soon before hard frost. It is not always possible to guess the weather and many craftsmen discount the frost danger to a vigorous hedge. It seems prudent, though, to avoid hard frost conditions. Frost dries out the cut surface of the wood and may burst the cell walls. Stems are more brittle under these conditions, more likely to break while being laid and less likely

to survive laying, although tree species vary in their hardiness and flexibility when frosted (pp 40-6).

If you must work during bitter weather several small fires alongside the hedgerow can significantly increase the temperature among the shrubs. Not too close, of course! Try to get the fires underway before beginning to lay the pleachers so the warmth will have some effect. Take care that they stay under control.

c   Be particularly careful about frost when laying a hedge with large old pleachers. These are liable to be brittle anyway, and respond less well to cutting. Frost will often kill them while more vigorous cut stems survive. It is best to lay them early or late in the season, when their sap is flowing. Early laying is probably best since it gives the stems a chance to harden off before winter and to resprout as soon as possible the next spring.

d   Work is difficult after heavy rains. It isn't pleasant to stand in full ditches (especially if they emanate from barns and farm outbuildings!) and hip waders have been known to be required when hedging after a storm. Work is hazardous when footing is bad, and it will be if the ditch or bank sides are saturated. Sodden soil is unstable, making it nearly impossible to carry out the subsidiary tasks of ditching and turfing. This work in particular should wait until the earth has dried a bit. Of course the surface may be wet while under the grass the soil remains dry, so the final decision to work or not is best made after inspecting the site.

Group Hedge Laying

Hedging is traditionally a solitary activity or one occasionally done in pairs. There are several reasons to keep to this pattern when possible. Axes and slashers are dangerous when used near other people and falling branches and flying thorns can catch nearby workers unaware. Hedge laying is a kind of puzzle which can be solved in many ways but only if two answers are not imposed at once. It's always aggravating to have a certain idea in mind as to where and how and when to lay a particular stem and then find it has been cut for you and put somewhere else. Finally, each individual has his own style which results in a distinctive hedge, slightly taller and thinner or shorter and thicker than others, with the pleachers at their particular angle and the brush trimmed in a particular way. People working in series along a stretch of hedge often result in noticeable and occasionally jarring changes of height etc. This is usually accentuated by the binding which dips and swells along the row.

Despite the solitary nature of the craft, conservation volunteers most often work in groups and with the right set-up hedgelaying can become a successful group activity. There are two approaches:

Approach A: Where a small labour force can finish the hedge in the required time.

The idea is to set up manageable teams which if possible do not have to meet. No more than three or four people should be employed on any distinct length of hedge. Where stakes and binders must be cut locally another two workers can be used, one to cut and sharpen stakes and the other to find and gather binders. The hedgerow lengths should be set off by gates, wide gaps which will have to be fenced, corners or other obvious breaks. Large hedgerow trees sometimes suppress the growth beneath them, making these sections unready to lay with the rest and creating convenient divisions on a long straight length of hedge.

Divide the labour so that only two people are actually cutting and laying at any one time. A pair can usually work well together, one person cutting while the other guides and lays each pleacher. It may be best to have one person work from the field side to get at stems which are hard to reach from the usual position. These two can start work while a third person finishes the initial trimming further down the row and the fourth collects and burns the cuttings. After a bit the third will be able to start placing stakes in the wake of the cutters and eventually bring up the heathering and do the final trimming up. It is usually best to switch positions from time to time so that everyone experiences all aspects of the job.

Approach B: Where a single length of hedge has no convenient breaks in it or where it requires more workers to finish it in time.

This is the situation in competition hedging where a hedge is divided into adjacent ten or eleven yard (10m) sections to be worked on by individual entrants. A neat and relatively uniform hedge can result, provided people are willing to co-operate!

Estimate the distance which each worker (or pair if cutting and laying it this way) will complete in the work day. To do this you need some experience of hedging in different conditions so that you can assess the particular hedge and group of volunteers. Ten to eleven yards is adequate for a craftsman hedger working alone although in very good conditions he may complete a full chain (22 yards, 20m) in a day. Mark off the estimated lengths with poles or any convenient indicators. This is to make it clear at what each worker must aim. Have a volunteer fire-tender/brush-remover for every few lengths so that cleaning-up can keep pace with laying.

Each worker or pair should work in the same direction, usually from left to right when facing the hedge from the near (ditch) side. They should be able to join up to their right hand neighbours at the end of the day provided one rule is followed. In competitions the rule is often stated 'the first two pleachers to be turned out', but for general work it should be the first group of pleachers which is 'turned out'. Best to save more than enough than to cut away all but two and make a lower hedge where the sections meet.

Each worker cuts his first pleachers on the left end of his section but instead of laying them normally, which would be impossible since he would be laying them into standing trees at the right end of the adjoining section, he turns them at a slight angle out to the sides. Here they sit, looking useless, until the worker on the left comes up to the end of his section and finds he is out of pleachers to fill the gap left by the laying of his last few stems. Ah! There they are - lying turned out to either side. Hopefully they are just right to finish off the section.

8 Laying the 'Standard' or Midlands Hedge

This chapter covers cutting, laying and binding techniques basic to laid hedges in general, leaving for the following chapter only those points needed to distinguish Welsh and South Western styles from the Midlands type and from each other.

When most people think of a 'typical' laid hedge, it is the Midlands type which they have in mind. The Midlands hedge extends from County Durham in the north through Yorkshire, Lincolnshire, Derbyshire and Nottinghamshire. It blends with Welsh styles in the border counties of Cheshire, Shropshire, Herefordshire and Worcestershire and reaches down to the northeast corner of Gloucestershire. Of course not all parts of these counties are hedged: the Pennine moorlands and the Lincoln fens, for example, are not. And fewer hedges are laid now than were even twenty years ago. The most expert examples to be found today occur in Warwickshire, Leicestershire and Nottinghamshire, the heart of Midlands hedge country.

It is convenient to describe the Midlands hedge as 'standard' not only because it springs to mind but because, compared with Welsh and South Western types, there is rather little variation in style other than that imposed by individual craftsmen. It is possible to refer to a true 'Midlands type', while in Wales for example there are at least four types with many variations within them.

Note, though, that there is one major variation, the so-called 'arable' style found mainly in the east Midlands and described by Pollard, Hooper and Moore (1974, p194). Here the pleachers are laid directly over the stools so that new growth comes up from the centre of the hedge, interlacing with the old. The resulting hedge is very dense but difficult to lay again. This method is especially useful on a young hedge, about ten years old, which can be subsequently trimmed to an A-shape. The hedge does not need to be laid again for a long time. Meanwhile crops are not shaded yet the barrier remains stockproof should the field be turned over periodically to grazing. The arable style rather closely resembles some of the Welsh styles although it developed in response to different needs.

Features of the Midlands Hedge

The Midlands hedge is designed primarily as a bullock fence. Typically, it is ditched along one side but lacks a bank or has only a slight bank formed by periodically mucking the ditch out onto the roots of the shrubs. Ditches, although perhaps at first boundary features associated with banks, later were used mainly for drainage on the frequently heavy soils of this region. So characteristic is the hedge-side ditch that it seems the style may have developed in response to the protection afforded by it to one side of the hedge.

Midlands hedges are asymmetrical in cross-section, with the brushy ends of the pleachers angled out into the field and away from the ditch. They are usually 4'-4'6" (1220mm-1370mm) tall, taller than other laid hedges, and are staked vertically down the centre line and bound along the top with binding or 'heathering'. The general idea is that cattle in the field or 'far' side are kept away from the shoots which spring up from the cut stools along the ditch or 'near' side. The brush angled into the field keeps beasts from pushing and rubbing on the hedge and the hedge's height keeps them from leaning over it. The stakes, with the pleachers 'woven' between them, make the whole hedge sturdy. The binding locks the pleachers down and keeps them from springing out of position. The pleachers should be live; the use of deadwood is frowned upon except to add strength to a very thin or gappy hedge. In other situations it is thought to serve no purpose and to inhibit the new growth.

A well-laid Midlands hedge makes an ideal horse jump, so it is not surprising that Hunts are now among the most active supporters of hedging competitions. Hunters prefer the stakes to be sawn off flat so as not to impale the horses. This would seem an example of a secondary function influencing minor stylistic points, but to the contrary Midlands craftsmen generally insist on lopping off their stakes with a sharp upward cut of the billhook in keeping with their artistic aim of 'making the white shine all one way' ie keeping all cut surfaces in the same plane.

In all Midlands hedging procedures the 'near side' of the hedge is the side with a ditch, and the 'far side' the side next to the field. Where there is no ditch either side can be chosen to be the near side. Remember, though, that it is this side which must be protected from grazing animals (p 52). See diagram next page.

Hedge Laying Procedure

It is best to estimate the length you expect to complete in a day's work and carry out the job on that length rather than to leave long stretches of hedge partly unfinished. When working alone, carry out each step in turn, with the exception of

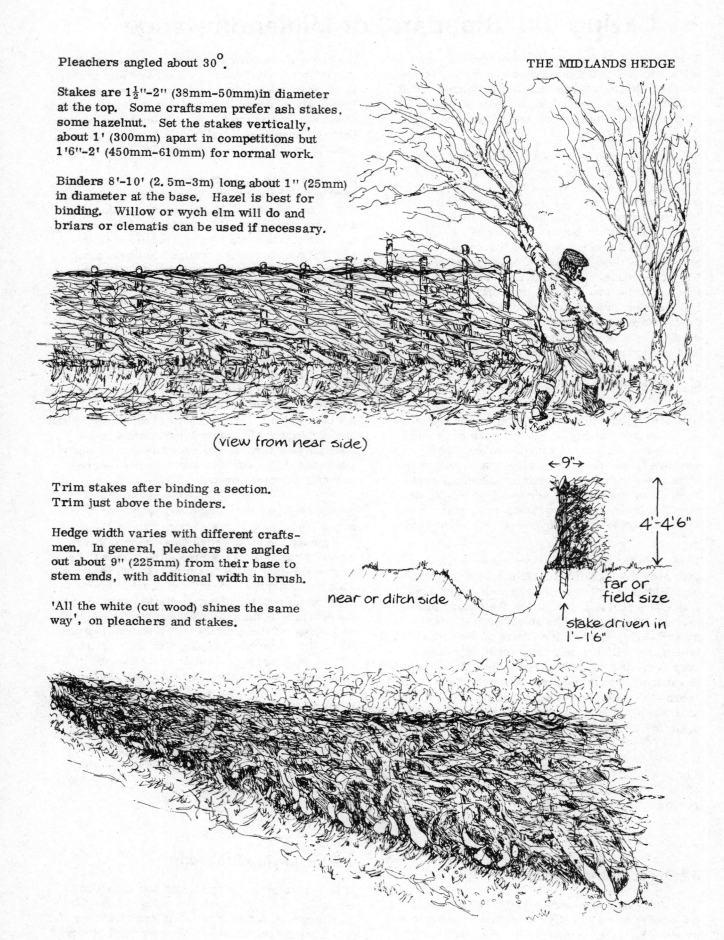

Pleachers angled about 30°.

Stakes are 1½"-2" (38mm-50mm)in diameter
at the top.   Some craftsmen prefer ash stakes,
some hazelnut.   Set the stakes vertically,
about 1' (300mm) apart in competitions but
1'6"-2' (450mm-610mm) for normal work.

Binders 8'-10' (2.5m-3m) long, about 1" (25mm)
in diameter at the base.   Hazel is best for
binding.   Willow or wych elm will do and
briars or clematis can be used if necessary.

(view from near side)

Trim stakes after binding a section.
Trim just above the binders.

Hedge width varies with different craftsmen.   In general, pleachers are angled
out about 9" (225mm) from their base to
stem ends, with additional width in brush.

'All the white (cut wood) shines the same
way', on pleachers and stakes.

←9"→

4'-4'6"

near or ditch side

far or
field size

stake driven in
1'-1'6"

pleaching and staking which proceed together, stakes being driven in a yard or two back of the advance pleachers. If trimmings are to be burned this can be carried on at the same time as the rest of the work. Modifications of the basic procedure for group work are discussed on page 71.

1 Set out stakes and binders. It is most convenient to drop off a bundle of each every 20'-30' (6m-10m) along the hedge where you can easily reach them as work progresses.

2 Remove rubbish. This includes old wire, sheet metal or rails put in to fill gaps, tins and bottles and anything else which will interfere with the work and possibly damage your tools. Pile rubbish for later disposal.

3 Preliminary trimming. Use a slasher to cut and pull brambles and vines out of the hedge. Cut out any elder plants. Elder suppresses other species through its vigorous growth and cannot be laid properly due to its brittle stem and soft pithy centre.

Do as much trimming as possible with an upward stroke. Cut with rather than directly across the grain of the branches for a neater, easier job.

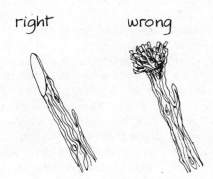

right   wrong

Trim back the brushy side growth along the near side of the hedge. Cut away enough to open up the stems for convenient pleaching and laying, but leave the tops of the trees bushy so that they form an effective barrier when laid. Ideally, trees for laying should be about 12' (3.6m) high and can be trimmed on the near side up to a height of about 8' (2.4m) with the slasher. If the trees are short, however, it is best to avoid trimming much off the sides until the trees are laid and in position, so that you can be sure that enough brush is left to make a dense living barrier.

Remove excess leafmould and bits of deadwood

from around the base of the trees to provide a clear cutting area. This can be done either before pleaching or as you go along, hooking the material out with slasher or billhook or trampling it in around the roots as convenient.

Throw the rubbish and trimmings where they will be easiest to deal with later. Keep combustibles and noncombustibles separate if you plan to burn the former. Where you pile trimmings depends on the site and on any arrangements you have with the land-owner, local council etc for collection of the material. In a typical hedge with ditch it is easiest to get a tractor along the field on the far side, so trimmings should be thrown over or pushed through into piles or a neat row on that side. Alongside a track, a canal tow-path or where the collector can easily get to the ditch edge, it is easiest to throw the trimmings behind you into piles or a row on the side of the ditch away from the hedge. Don't just leave things where they fall, particularly in the ditch, because this makes a laborious job later picking up the loose bits by hand, unless the whole ditch is to be cleaned out. It is especially important to collect thorny twigs and small bits of barbed wire which may otherwise injure livestock when stepped on.

4 Cut and lay the pleachers. Points 4-7 are dealt with in detail below.

5 Stake the laid hedge.

6 Bind (heather) the hedge.

7 Trim the stakes for an even finish.

8 Final trimming. This produces a well-finished look and keeps cattle from rubbing against projecting stiff stems.

Use a billhook to cut off spriggy bits sticking out on the near side or top of the hedge. Trim stems near a joint or knot: new side shoots grow from just below the joint nearest the cut tip so it does no good to leave a long dead end beyond this joint. (See diagram on next page).

Trim off the thin ends of the binders and their side shoots if they have any. Check along the pleacher stumps to make sure that all stubs or 'ears' have been trimmed off clean and that wood chips or dirt are not obscuring the cuts. Take a look back along what you've

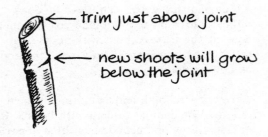

trim just above joint

new shoots will grow below the joint

finished.   All the inner 'white' of the cut stems and stakes should 'shine the same way'.

9   Collect rubbish and trimmings for removal to a rubbish tip or burn them.

10   If stock are in the field, make sure that any gaps left at the end of the day are filled with stout deadwood branches wedged into place between laid and unlaid sections of the hedge or with barbed wire, rails etc.

11   Protect the hedge as necessary from the time laying is finished through the next one or two growing seasons (p 52).

12   Clean the ditch if this is needed.   Do this after laying is completed along the whole hedge.   Cut back the ditch to reveal any land drain outlets.   Dig the bottom out to 6" (150mm) below the outlets.   The ditch should have a sloping profile, wider at the top than bottom, so that when it carries water the banks remain stable.

Soil cut from the ditch is traditionally banked around the stools of the hedge, leaving about 2" (50mm) of stool showing.   Some workers say the soil soon falls back into the ditch and that instead it should be heaped along the edge of the ditch away from the hedge or spread over the adjoining field.   This may allow weeds from the spoil to invade the field and so should not be done on cropped land or pasture.

Cutting and Laying, Staking and Binding

Different craftsmen have different terms for the work described here.   For clarity, we define 'cutting' as the partial severing of stems in order to bend them over.   To 'lay' or 'layer' is to actually bend the stems and position them at the correct angle.   The stems which are treated in this way are known here as 'pleachers'.

WHY THE PLEACHERS LIVE

The stem of a tree has several divisions which can be seen in cross section.

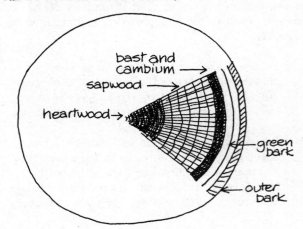

bast and cambium

sapwood

heartwood

green bark

outer bark

The bark protects the tree from fire, frost, predators and disease.   The bast is a thin layer formed of tiny channels which carry sugar sap downward from the leaves into the roots.   The cambium is also very thin and is the part of the stem which actually undergoes cell division and growth.   The sapwood supports the tree and carries the ascending sap with its inorganic nutrients from the roots to the leaves.   Finally, in older trees of most species, the inner sapwood dies to form heartwood as the tree grows bigger.

Hedgerow species are mainly hardy, especially when well-established but not aged.   Some, such as the thorns, will frequently regrow from the base even when completely severed.   But the idea when laying a hedge is to make a live barrier of cut and laid pleachers.   The laid pleachers will survive as long as the necessary nutrient flow can still take place from roots to tip. Bark, bast, cambium and at least a little sapwood must be left, joined in a thin strip of stem from which the upper portions can draw nourishment.   This is what hedgers mean when they say you 'have to leave the bark and a bit more' when cutting through the tree, and on the other hand, when laying it, 'if you break the bark at the back - if it kinks up - the stick will die'.

There is more to successful cutting and laying than this, though.   Pleachers must be laid flat or at an upward angle - never downward - no matter how tempting it is to cut a bit high and bring the stem down to fill in the base of the hedge.   'Sap never runs downhill,' so downsloping pleachers soon die back, defeating the object of a live hedge.   Another important consideration is the long-range health of the trees at their roots and bases.   Cutting and laying is major surgery

- it weakens the plants and opens them up to infection and rotting. Everything possible must be done to insure a neat, 'sterile' operation when cutting and to cleanly trim the protruding stubs so that water cannot collect in the cuts. This is detailed below.

FROM WHICH SIDE TO WORK?

Midlands hedges are asymmetrical, with most of the cutting done on the near side and the brush angled out on the far or field side. Whenever possible, then, stand on the near side to work. If you stand on the far side you will find the brushy ends getting in your way and, worse, you will be tempted to cut and lay the trees nearest you and chop out the ones farther away, which in fact are the ones to lay since they are better protected against livestock.

Another advantage of working from the near side is that, if it is ditched, you can stand in the ditch or on its slope and cut the trees near ground level with much less bending than if you stand level with the hedge itself. At times the ditch may be awkwardly steep and deep or right against the hedge. Or it may be running full, in which case you will need to wear wellies or waders or modify your stance. But it is still best to work from the near side unless your perch is dangerously precarious.

Where the hedge has large gaps you may find it easy to change sides to suit the individual pleacher. When laying 'from the root' or disposing of large stools (see below) you may have to work around the base. Generally, though, it is energy-consuming and entangling to cross the hedge line frequently.

WHICH DIRECTION TO LAY?

If you are right handed it is easiest to cut the pleachers from the right side and steady them and guide them into position with the left hand. This means that as you face the hedge you begin at its left end and lay the pleachers working along to your right.

If you are left handed do the opposite, cutting from the left, guiding the pleachers with your right hand, and working from your right along to the left.

When more than one person is laying the hedge, all must work in the same direction. In this way different sections can merge into one another (how this is done is explained later). If laying is carried out in opposite directions there will be gaps in some sections and a tangle of conflicting pleachers in others.

If left and right handed people work on the same hedge the 'odd man out' should accommodate by working from the field side. This is easier than laying wrong-handed from the same side as the others, unless he is fortunate enough to be ambidextrous.

Some craftsmen say you should lay 'uphill and upstream' when hedging on a slope. Others say this is of no importance. The argument for uphill laying seems to have some point. Hedge shrubs tend to grow straight up and on a marked slope the angle between the stem and the ground is less on the uphill than on the downhill side. If the stems are laid downhill they must be bent over more than if laid uphill, in order to lie at the proper angle in relation to the slope and stakes, with a greater risk of breaking. Stems laid this way also tend to spring up, making it difficult to keep the pleachers in place and putting more strain on the binding.

LAYING ON A SLOPE

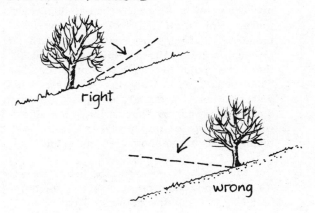

This argument is appreciated by Welsh hedgers, who frequently have to hedge on a slope and who seldom use binding. To them a downsloping hedge 'looks wrong' - something that no good craftsmen tolerates. Often the slope forces them to lay the hedge 'wrong-handed' in order to lay uphill while still working from the near side. With practice many have become ambidextrous at this task.

GENERAL PRINCIPLES OF CUTTING AND LAYING

Hedgerows are seldom accommodating. They are either thin and gappy or dense and tangled. Trees never lie in a single straight row. Most hedges are originally planted in a double staggered row and over time some trees die or are suppressed by their more vigorous neighbours. Suckers spring up to the sides of the parent trees and new individuals seed in around the plantings, further confusing the planting line.

If the hedge is sparse, every possible stem must be laid including those normally cut out, with the exception of elder which is always removed. Gap-closing expedients are described on pages 83-5.

The following points summarise the strategy when there is adequate material for cutting and laying:

a   Cut out trees which are well out of line of the original hedgerow plantings, especially those growing from the ditch side. To use these as pleachers would encourage the further widening of the hedge, with a weakening of the main line plants, and make it more difficult to form an effective laid barrier the next time. Trees growing from the ditch side also tend to break down the bank and clog the ditch.

b   Cut out all deadwood. This includes dead standing stems and old pleachers which have been gradually suppressed by vigorous upward-growing shoots. Excess deadwood makes it more difficult to lay the new pleachers and may suppress new growth, although some craftsmen heatedly dispute this latter point (eg those who practice double brushing in Wales). Of course it is better to insert a moderate number of sturdy deadwood pleachers than to leave a hedge which is gappy or low in places due to insufficient or too short live material.

c   Cut out excess livewood in the hedge line. As with deadwood, too many live pleachers tend to suppress new growth. Cut out smoothwood species in preference to thorns if the thorns are suitably positioned for laying. But keep more than enough stems until you are sure they aren't needed. You must cut out enough stems to allow access to the chosen pleachers but nothing is worse than finding yourself with an accidently severed or unsuitable pleacher and nothing to replace it with. Once it is safely laid and in position, the rest of the surrounding livewood can be dispatched.

d   Use as many separate plants for pleachers as possible, within the limits set above. It often happens that you can choose between laying several of the stems of a multiple-stemmed tree or entirely cutting out all but one or two of the stems and laying the adjacent plant as well. Choose the latter alternative. In this way you encourage the survival of more rootstock and help the long term

survival of an adequately dense hedge. Otherwise the hedge tends increasingly to be made up of a few many-stemmed trees with large gaps between, which makes for much more difficult maintenance in the future.

Choosing which of the multiple stems to use is discussed on page 82.

e   When you want to lay more than one pleacher at a given point in the hedgerow, lay the near side pleacher or the pleacher growing from a hollow first. This forms the bottom part of the barrier, effective against sheep. Next lay the far side pleachers or those growing on hummocks to form the upper part of the barrier, effective against cattle. This is easier and works better than if the pleachers are laid in the opposite order.

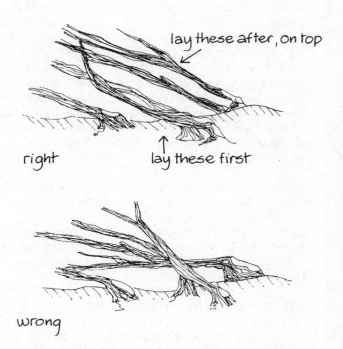

right   lay these first

wrong

f   Before cutting and laying any pleacher make sure it is free of entanglement. Tug the upper part of the stem. If it is hung up, cut it free with a slasher. You may have to cut off branches with axe or billhook if they are seriously tangled but try to keep enough brash near the end for the pleacher to be effective.

You must be able to lower the stem gently into position once it is cut. Otherwise it may twist, kink or break off. Make sure you cut and lay the stems in the right order Cut away unwanted stems which may interfere with laying.

g   Cut each pleacher near but not at ground
level, so that the stem can bend over at a
point more than 1" (25mm) but less than
about 4" (100mm) off the ground.

Trees seldom regrow right from the cut
surface but rather from a point about an
inch below this, due to the wood just under
the cut being killed by frost and water pene-
tration. This is why at least an inch of
stump is necessary for proper sprouting.
An exception is blackthorn which tends to
sucker from roots to the side of the cut stem.

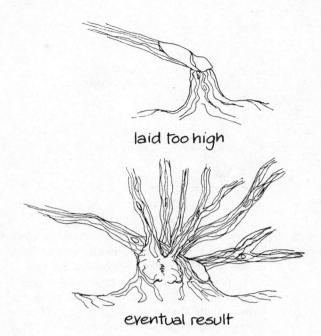

laid too high

eventual result

If you must cut high, for example when you
have a thick pleacher and lack a power saw
to help cut it at the base, you can encourage
the stump to sprout near the base by cutting
out a notch like this:

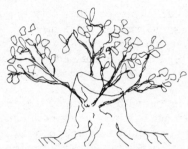

normal regrowth

regrowth on Blackthorn

When 'laying from the root' the cut may be
below original ground level but the earth is
dug away to expose enough root or stump for
sprouting (p 83).

It is tempting to cut too high, especially on
old trees where the stem may be thick or
gnarled at the base. High cutting is a mistake
for three reasons:
(a) Stems laid too high may leave a gap at
    the base of the hedge.
(b) Stems laid so that they angle downward
    will not survive, due to the sap flow
    being cut off at the bend.
(c) Stems laid high will sprout high. The
    next time someone has to lay the hedge
    he will have even more difficulty laying
    from the base. The hedger's curse is on
    the previous worker who left him a job
    like this:

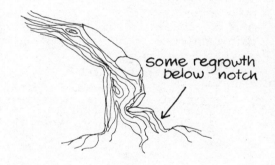

some regrowth
below notch

CUTTING TECHNIQUES

These are described and illustrated for a right
handed worker.

Method 1: Billhook or axe

Use a billhook on stems up to about 3" (75mm) in
diameter at the base.

a   Cut at a sharp downward angle with, not
    across, the grain. This applies to all
    cutting with a billhook, and all cutting with
    an axe unless the intention is to chop through
    a thick stem. (See diagram next page).

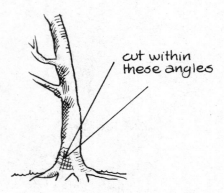

cut within these angles

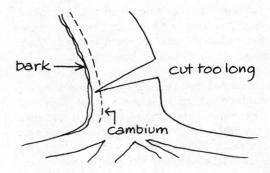

bark → cut too long

cambium

b   Begin the cut so that it will end at the correct point rather more than ¾ of the way through the stem. Thin stems should be cut to 1"-2" (25mm-50mm) above ground level. Thicker (eg 4"-6", 100mm-150mm diameter) stems should be cut to about 3"-4" (75mm-100mm) above ground level so that the stub can be trimmed properly.

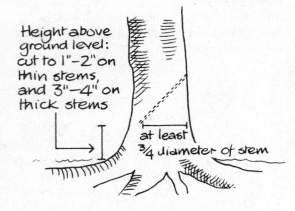

Height above ground level: cut to 1"-2" on thin stems, and 3"-4" on thick stems

at least ¾ diameter of stem

Cutting to the exact point requires skill and practice as well as an ability to judge the flexibility and strength of each stem. You must be able to lay the stem over without wrenching it or causing the cut to split downward into the base. On the other hand you must not sever the living layer or leave the pleacher hanging by a weak strip so that it breaks under stress or under the weight of pleachers laid on top of it.

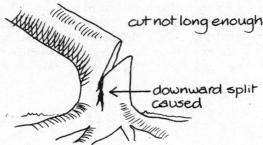

cut not long enough

downward split caused

c   When you near the point where you want the cut to stop gently pull the stem with the left hand down and to the left to open up the mouth of the cut. Then continue cutting and pulling at the same time until the pleacher can be eased into position. This keeps the tool from binding in the cut and gives you greatest control over the pleacher's descent.

When laying with an axe you will probably have to cut part way using both hands, then stop to test the pleacher, then cut further with both hands being ready to stop so that you can grab the pleacher with your left hand, support it and lower it.

d   If the pleacher does not lay easily with gentle pulling, place the billhook or axe blade in the cut and twist the tool with a wrist action, helping to lever the stem over and to extend the cut slightly while controlling the fall with the left hand.

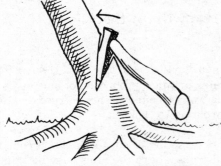

e   On thicker stems it helps to make a tension-releasing cut first, beginning at a point below that of the final cut. The lower cut should not extend below the level at which the final cut will end.

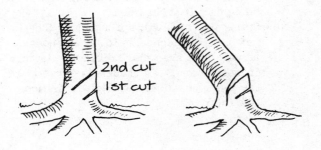

2nd cut
1st cut

f   Trim the protruding stub after the pleacher is laid and in position. Begin the cut about 1" (25mm) above ground level and cut upward at a 45° angle or more to end at the point where the pleacher has been bent over. The idea is to completely and cleanly remove the stub so that water cannot collect in the cut. Water in the cut may gradually rot the stool and kill the new shoots. In addition, sharp projecting stubs are extremely dangerous to stock. Cows have been known to bleed to death after slipping and falling on an untrimmed stub while trying to push through the hedge.

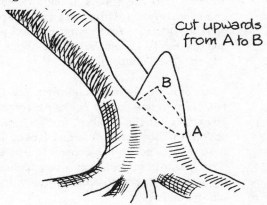

cut upwards from A to B

If your initial cut to lay the stem has ended at the correct point you will be able to trim the stub at the proper angle. But if you have laid too low you will have to cut the stub across the grain, battering the stem and splintering the base. Try to trim with the fewest number of strokes. Thin stems can be trimmed with one blow but gnarled old pleachers require quite a bit of axework. If your tools are sharp the job will be clean, and the cleaner the job the better the survival potential of the plant.

Method 2: Saw and billhook or axe

This is the easiest method for workers with limited billhook and axe skills.

Some craftsmen claim that trees treated this way survive less readily and sprout less well due to the shattering of the grain when sawn. This can be corrected by paring off the sawn surface afterward with billhook or axe. Some craftsmen dislike using saws purely because a skilled worker can do without and because they are not used traditionally. Others, though, use a power saw to fell or lay large pleachers, feeling that the time saved outweighs the disadvantages of noise, fumes and shattered grain.

a   Saw the stem directly across an inch or

two (25mm-50mm) above the ground, stopping at the point where you want the stem to bend over.

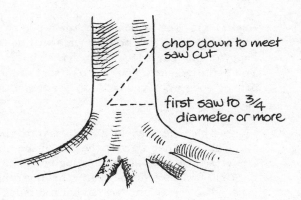

chop down to meet saw cut

first saw to ¾ diameter or more

b   Cut out a wedge with the billhook or, if it is a thick stem, with an axe and ease the stem over. Cut down past the saw cut before laying. Use the billhook or axe as a lever if necessary. You will probably have to extend the downward cut slightly below the level of the cross cut in order to bend the pleacher, but try not to chop too vigorously or the cut will tend to run down below ground level. Also, try to avoid hacking the sawn stump.

c   Trim off the stump with billhook or axe in order to clean up the sawn wood. This is possible only if your tool is very sharp since you must cut across the grain. If it is not, dispense with this step rather than further splintering the wood.

LAYING AND STAKING THE PLEACHERS

a   Lower each pleacher gently into place, trying not to twist or shake it in the process. Sap will not flow properly to a sharply twisted stem. If you have to shake or bash the pleacher into position you may break or tear it off the stump.

b   Pleachers should be laid at about a 25°-45° angle upward. The angle is determined to some extent by the number, location and length of pleachers. Where there is a gap, pleachers should be laid low to fill the opening at ground level and other pleachers brought in above at a steeper angle if possible. Where the pleacher stems are fairly bare between the base and brushy top they again should be laid at a lesser angle in order to make best use of the brush on the far side of the hedge. Alternatively the hedge can be made taller, with some pleachers laid low and some laid at the proper angle.

Avoid laying the pleachers at too steep an angle because if you do the hedge will be too gappy to form an adequate livestock barrier. You will also end up cutting off most of the brushy ends when you trim off the top of the hedge.

c   Lay the pleachers about 9" (225mm) off the stumps. In other words, the end of the main stems or branches should be angled out into the field by this amount, as in the diagram on page 74. Pleachers angled out too much make the hedge unnecessarily wide and weaken the barrier. If they are not angled out at all they are difficult to set between the stakes and make too thin a barrier.

d   After the first few pleachers have been laid, position the stakes and drive them in with a mell, wooden billet or sledgehammer. The positioning of the stakes can be shown most easily in a diagram.

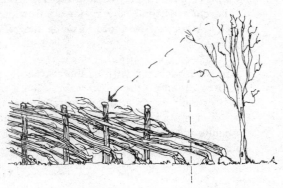

The arrow shows how the thin, brushy ends of the pleachers should reach to a few stakes. The vertical dotted line shows where another stake is ready to be added. It should be pushed between the laid stems and driven home.

Weave the thin, whippy ends of each pleacher around the last few of the stakes which it reaches so that each pleacher is held firmly in position with its brushy end angled out into the field. Where a stem forks into several main branches these can be criss-crossed for a better grip on the stakes. Just be sure most of the branches project on the field side where the brush is needed.

Depending on the diameter of the trees and the way they lie when laid, you may want to add two or three stakes at once rather than one at a time. Just be sure not to cramp your work space for laying the next pleachers, and try not to knock the stakes about when laying. (See diagram below.)

When driving stakes, stop when you feel real resistance due to rocks or roots. If you try to hit the stake in farther you may knock it badly out of line and loosen it. If the stake is not in far enough to be fairly firm, take it out, shift it a few inches and try again. Try to keep it in line with the other stakes.

SPECIAL PROBLEMS WHEN CUTTING AND LAYING

Multiple-stemmed trees

How many of the stems you use as pleachers depends on the supply of pleachers from other nearby plants and the actual position of the stems on the stool (see point d, page 78). Cut away unwanted stems before laying the chosen pleachers (occasionally you may need to lay a pleacher first in order to gain cutting access to a stem which you plan to sever). Use the easiest stems to cut and lay, as long as they are sturdy enough to make good pleachers. Cut out thin and weak stems as well as old, very thick stems where you have a choice.

far side

Pleachers 'woven' between stakes with bushy ends into field

(top view)

near side

Line of stakes just to the far side of the main line of stools

position of next stake

Where you plan to use several stems, follow the usual procedure: lay the left hand and near side stems first and lowest and the far side stems on top or to the far side. Modify this as needed to avoid hang-ups and make for easiest cutting.

Large stools

These are caused by the plant having been cut and laid too high, probably more than once. Each time this happens, the base thickens and sprouts shoots which, if laid in their turn, make the stool a gnarled and bulky impediment to proper laying. Resist the temptation to carry on the bad practice. Where you can afford to sacrifice the whole plant in favour of adjacent, better pleachers, it is best to cut it out completely. Frequently, though, this would open up too big a gap or else leave a gap unpleached further down the hedge and the only choice is to lay the plant near ground level.

Inspect the stool. Can you sever it vertically into several distinct plants, each with root and stem? This may be laborious but is the best way to get manageable portions which can be laid from the root (see below). First cut out unwanted stems and rotten, cankerous parts of the stool. This may make it easier to subdivide the remaining stump. This is difficult work due to the twisted, complex grain of the wood and the awkward cutting positions forced on you by the location of the stems and of other trees near the stool. Axe work is easiest, if you can handle the tool ambidextrously and if it is very sharp. A chain saw is useful in these situations, but cut very slowly and carefully, taking out bits of the stool rather than cutting straight through it, in order not to bind the chain in the twisted grain. Note too that you are likely to encounter stones and earth trapped in the stool with consequent damage to the chain.

Laying from the root

Use this technique when cutting and laying old, large-stemmed trees which may have gone rotten and cankered or brittle where you would normally cut them. Use it also where the stem is 'pinched' and is likely to break off if layed in the normal way. And lay from the root where the tree has been previously cut and laid too high and you want to have it sprout again near ground level.

Some people think that it harms the hedge to lay from the root because root wood does not shoot as well as stem wood and because frost is more likely to harm root wood where it has been exposed. Where there is no alternative to laying from the root, take the precautions of not working in mid-winter when sharp frosts are most likely and of covering the root with earth

below the point of cutting after the pleacher is laid.

Follow this procedure:

1   With a spade, cut away earth around the base of the plant as necessary to expose the junctions of the main lateral roots and the stem.

2   Inspect the stool. Try to find a good strong thick root, attached to the chosen pleacher, which runs into the ground at a distinct angle to the line of laying. This root will serve as both anchor and pivot to the pleacher as it is being layed, and afterwards will provide as direct a flow of nutrients to the pleacher as possible.

3   With the axe or bow saw, sever the small roots on the side towards which the pleacher will be laid. This should free the pleacher to bend in that direction. Sever, in the course of cutting and laying, any root other than the anchor root which appears to prevent the right movement of the pleacher.

4   Cut the pleacher in the normal way. Aim the cut so that it splits the anchor root approximately in half. Cut down to ground level, testing the pleacher as you work and being ready to support it if it starts to fall.

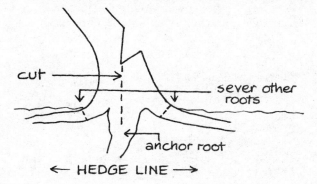

5   Gently lower the pleacher into position, continuing the cut little by little as needed to lay the stem. The grain of the root will twist as the pleacher is laid but it should not break.

6   Cut away the unwanted remains of the stool.

Laying back to fill gaps

Where there is a gap or 'shard' which cannot be filled by pleachers further up the hedgerow (to the right, if you are working from left to right) it may be possible to lay back from a position on the left of the gap.

First, however, you must work up to the gap from the left using as many stems as necessary to carry the hedge to this point with adequate pleachers. Only use remaining 'excess' stems to lay back to the right.

Method A:

This method requires great skill and judgement but results in the best new growth to fill the gap. It also preserves the uniform look of the laid pleachers and avoids entanglement between pleachers laid in opposite directions.

Select strong, thick pleachers to lay into the gap. With luck they will have advantageously placed bends or branches for the required laying angles.

1   Lay the stem at ground level, as usual, but from the opposite side. In other words, cut on the left side and lay the tree to the right. Lay it along the ground to fill the bottom of the gap. If necessary, lay from the root or cut away the weaker roots to do this. Lay the pleacher in line with the hedge rather than angled out to the field side as normal.

2   Now cut and lay the upper end of the pleacher back to the left, ie in the usual direction of laying. Cut the stem on the right side, being careful not to let the cut split too far down. Angle the pleacher slightly to the far side as is normal.

Pleacher laid to fill gap

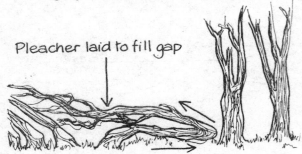

Make this second cut at the point where pleachers layed from the right will fill the lower part of the gap and still provide material to finish off the upper part of the hedge at this point. If possible this should be where the pleacher almost reaches the right side of the gap, so that pleachers laid from the right can be laid at the normal angle rather than having to lie flat to fill the bottom of the gap. The important thing in any case it to fill the gap and keep adequate brush on the field side even if the pleachers are angled rather irregularly. If you have selected the pleacher well, this point will

correspond to a place where the stem naturally bends back to the left or where it has some branches going leftwards. This allows the stem to be laid with less stress and risk of breakage than would otherwise be the case.

3   Lay the pleachers on the right side of the gap to finish filling the gap and to come over the left-side pleacher in the usual way.

Method B:

This is easier but less satisfactory than method A because it requires pleachers to be laid in opposite directions one to another. Pleachers tend to become tangled while being laid and the neat look of the finished hedge is destroyed.

To close the gap from the left, cut and lay pleachers exactly opposite to the normal way, ie cut them on the left side and lay them over to the right, across the gap. Angle them into the field in the usual way. Cut in the usual order: lower and near side pleachers first to fill the lower part of the gap. Then go to the right of the gap and lay stems from this side to the left to finish filling the gap. Where these pleachers cross the others, they should be laid on top to fill the upper part of the gap. Use each pleacher to best advantage, even if it means laying some of the left side stems, then some of those on the right, then other left side stems and so on depending on their shape and position in the hedgerow. The main thing is to fill the gap effectively.

Finishing the hedge

Where the hedge finishes against another hedgerow which is not ready to be laid, or against a gatepost etc, there will be a gap above and to the right of the last pleacher in line. This can be filled by laying back into the gap as in method B (above), provided there are sufficient pleachers to maintain the hedge at the required height and thickness.

Unless there is a gap of several feet between the last pleacher in line and the desired end of the hedgerow, the stems to be laid into the end gap should not be the last ones but some of those a few feet to the left. Select the pleachers to avoid a sharp 'parting of the ways' and resultant gap where the pleachers are laid both ways from the same point.

Rooting pleachers

Pleaching across a gap does not in itself ensure that the gap will permanently close. For this new shoots, and therefore new rootstock, must be placed in the gap. Where it is impractical to plant new trees, pleachers can be encouraged to root if they are laid in the following way:

1   Lay the pleacher from the root, ie select a healthy, strong but not too old root which is angled properly to anchor the pleacher. Sever all other roots, from which young shoots will spring.

2   Cut the pleacher so that it lies close to the ground with some part touching the earth. Clear away any grass at the point of contact and dig out a shallow trough so that the stem is half buried in the earth just at the bends which lend themselves to the purpose.

Alternatively, cut a notch in the top of the pleacher where it lies close to the ground and heap earth over the notched section, burying it.

3   If the weight of the pleacher is not enough to hold it in position, peg it down so that it is in firm contact with the ground.

Roots should develop where the stem is buried. When the hedge is next laid the stem can be cut through between these roots and the old, creating a new and independent plant which in later years can be cut and laid to best advantage.

BINDING

Binding or heathering helps finish off the hedge and also holds down the pleachers. Unless bound, the pleachers tend to spring out of position and push the tops of the stakes out of line. By the time the binding rots, the hedge has consolidated with new growth and the binding is no longer needed.

Good hedgers take pride in their binding, selecting the best hazel wands that they can find for the job. Other materials such as sweet chestnut stems, willow, clematis or even briars can be substituted, but hazel lasts longest. Barbed wire should not be used, since it tends to disintegrate before the hedge is ready for cutting and laying again and to fall out of sight among the stools. Then when the hedge is laid the wire bits soon blunt the hedger's tools.

Binders should be about 8'-10' (3m) long and about 1" (25mm) in diameter at the base, tapering evenly to the whippy ends. You can use slightly larger or smaller binders according to what is available, but thicker binders may have to be woven in a 2-rod pattern and thinner ones in a 4-rod pattern. Either way they will not look as good as the 3-rod pattern normally used.

Binders should not be too dry. They need to be flexible and to hold the position into which they are twisted. They should be straight and free of kinks and side branches. You can trim off small side stems as you work.

Beddall (1950, p 71) describes a method of binding which we have never seen but which might work well where hazel is plentiful in the hedge. He associates it with hedgers who use live stakes, again a practice which we have not seen in the Midlands although some Welsh hedgers do this (p 98). Beddall says:

> Tall slender shoots should be left standing at regular intervals to be used as hethers or binders when the other shoots are laid. These tall rods should then be woven in and out of the upright shoots, placing them in the opposite direction to the laid shoots. These will then bind the hedge into a solid living fence which has no dead wood in it at all.

The usual method is similar but uses cut binders and dead stakes.

Craftsmen hedgers do their binding so quickly and neatly that the process is hard to follow. The binding is usually said to be 'woven' or 'twisted' around the stakes, but one hedger told us that

'it's really more of a tight roll than a twist'.
The binders are made to keep tightly together like
strands of rope.

Procedure

Note that in the diagrams illustrating binding
procedure, the binders are shown as if loosely
woven to make the pattern clear. In practice the
binders should be woven or rolled as tightly as
possible.

1   If you have been working from left to right,
     from the near side of the hedge, begin
     binding at the left.   You bind against the
     lie of the pleachers.

2   Anchor the butt end of the first binder by
     pushing it firmly into the top of the hedge
     a little to the left of the first stake.   Bring
     it in front of this stake and behind the
     second stake.

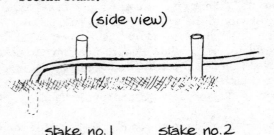

(side view)

stake no. 1   stake no. 2

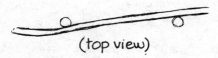

(top view)

3   Insert the butt ends of two binders under the
     first binder so that their butts are on the
     far side of the first stake.   They will lie
     against the near side of the second stake.

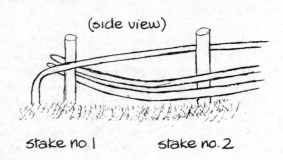

(side view)

stake no. 1   stake no. 2

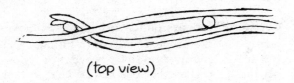

(top view)

4   'Roll' the first binder under the second pair
     between stakes two and three, so that it
     emerges in front of stake three while the
     other two binders pass behind stake three.
     (See diagrams 4, 5, and 6 on next page.)

5   Insert the butt end of a fourth binder under
     the others so that the butt rests against the
     far side of stake two and the remainder lies
     in front of stake three.   Roll it and the loose
     end of the first binder over the other two, so
     that the fourth and first binders twist over
     the second and third and pass behind stake
     four.   The second and third binders will lie
     in front of stake four.

6   Insert the butt end of the fifth binder under the
     others so that the butt rests against the far
     side of stake three and the remainder lies in
     front of stake four.   Roll it over the first and
     fourth binders, taking the second and third
     binders with it.   At about this point you may
     come to the ends of the first, second and
     third binders but carry them as far as they go.
     The fifth binder should pass over the fourth
     and lie behind stake five, while the fourth
     binder lies in front of stake five.

7   Insert the sixth binder under the others so
     that it rests against the far side of stake four
     and comes in front of stake five.   Roll it and
     the fifth binder across the other binders and
     bring the others in front so that they lie
     respectively behind and in front of stake six.

8   Continue in the same way, adding one new
     binder at each stake.

9   At the end of the row, leave the ends of the
     last binders hanging to the right of the last
     stake if you plan to add more stakes later.
     If you have finished the hedgerow, trim off
     the ends of the binders a little to the right
     of the last stake.

10   Walk back along the hedge to the left, tamping
     down the binding with the handle of your
     billhook as you go.   Try to make it as level,
     even and tight as possible, so that it really
     grips the stakes and holds the hedge down.

11   Trim off any projecting small ends of binders
     and any side shoots, for neatness.

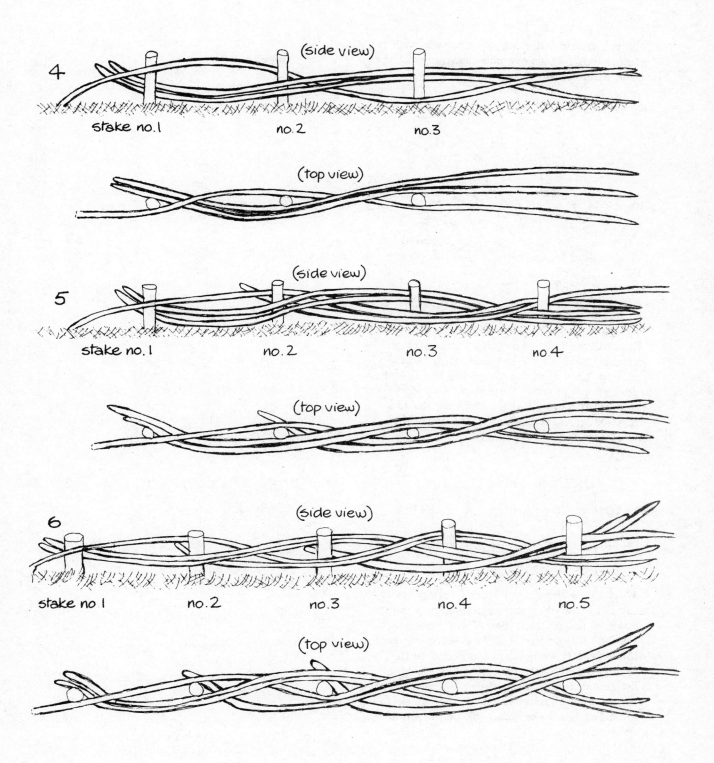

4

(side view)

stake no.1 no.2 no.3

(top view)

5

(side view)

stake no.1 no.2 no.3 no.4

(top view)

6

(side view)

stake no.1 no.2 no.3 no.4 no.5

(top view)

TRIMMING THE STAKES

Trim off the stake tops after binding a section of
hedge. The following procedure describes the
method used in the Midlands. Note that Welsh
hedgers usually cut off stakes with a saw (p 90).
Sawing may be the easiest method for volunteers,
but the billhook achieves a cleaner, neater and
more rot-resistant finish on the fairly thin stakes
used in Midlands hedges.

Procedure

1   Hold a short billet or stout stick behind the
stake to be trimmed. Rest the billet on the
binding. It may help to angle it from the
back of the first stake to the front of the next
one in line. The billet supports the stake
against the blow and ensures a clean cut.

2   Strike the stake sharply with the billhook.

The cut should slope steeply upwards with the grain. Skilled hedgers can usually sever the stake with one blow.

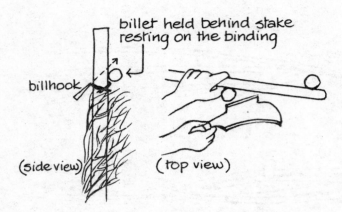

3   If the stake is a bit too thick to cut straight through, hold the billet behind it as before and chop a notch in the near side of the stake. First chop upwards, then down, to keep from splitting the stake. Then cut the top off as usual, aiming the blow to carry through the bottom face of the notch.

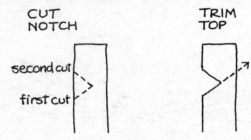

4   Work along the row of stakes, always hold-ing the billhook at the same angle as the angle of the cut surfaces of the pleacher stools. These surfaces face obliquely rather than directly away from the hedge so that they are more noticeable looking along the hedge one way than the other. The general impression should be that all the cut surfaces, including the stake tops, 'shine the same way'.

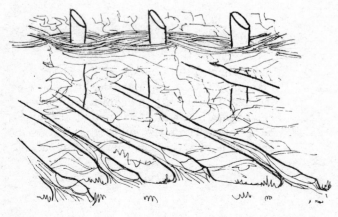

9 Laying Welsh and South Western Hedges

Basic techniques for cutting and laying are the same as for all types of hedges. In this chapter all methods and procedures are the same as for the Midlands hedge unless otherwise stated.

For convenience, banking and turfing, which are important aspects of hedging in both Wales and the South West, are discussed separately in the next chapter. Banking and turfing should always be carried out before cutting and laying the hedge but after clearing rubbish and trimming back the sides to make the work easier.

General Features of Welsh Hedges

The many and varied styles of Welsh hedges seem at first to defy classification. Each county claims a hedging tradition of its own. In some areas the 'county style' may be supplanted by quite different local forms. And on the local level it is often hard to tell if a particular hedge is representative of its area or is a single craftsman's idiosyncratic blending of styles into a new combination.

The border counties add to the variety by mixing elements of Welsh and Midlands hedges. In general, Monmouthshire hedges can be planted firmly in the Welsh camp whereas the hedges of Cheshire, Shropshire and Hereford tend to be 'thin' versions of the Midlands hedge, often ditched but sometimes on the flat or on a bank.

Despite this confusion, Welsh hedges show certain characteristic differences from the typical Midlands hedge. Some of these differences are shared by border county hedges, but not consistently. Whenever 'Welsh hedges' are discussed as a group one should mentally add 'and some border county hedges'.

Welsh hedges are designed primarily as sheep fences. Because of this they are usually dense but not necessarily very high, depending on the local breed of sheep. More or less deadwood is invariably added to the laid hedge to form a blockade to the sheep until the hedge has regrown. On sites where snow blows and drifts, hedges must be made strong enough to resist lateral pressure, and often these hedges are also rounded to let snow slide off to the sides rather than sitting on top and possibly crushing the hedge. In other parts of Wales, especially in the southern lowlands, the weather is mild and hedges can be left unstaked, squat and square atop high banks. By contrast, in the northeast the banks are low or nonexistant and the hedges are laid nearly as tall as in the Midlands. Where mixed farming is the rule, as it is in the northeast and in the border counties, types showing characteristics of both the sheep fence and the Midlands hedge are used to keep in both sheep and cattle

Many Welsh hedges have no ditch. Instead most are built on a distinct bank varying from a few inches to more than 4' (1.2m) in height. The banks are in some localities known as 'ditches' but this does not change their function. Although the field may be drained, the bank itself keeps the hedge out of water in the wettest climate and in fact measures must be taken to keep the plants from drying out. On steep hillsides the banks often have one face only and serve to prevent the loss of soil downhill, rather as do terraces. In the mildest parts of Wales, as in the South West, the banks become dominant and the hedges are much reduced in size. High banks provide the best defence against wind, a major factor when farming near the Atlantic.

Many Welsh hedges are said to be either 'single' or 'double brushed'. Single brushed hedges have the pleachers laid mainly from one side of the hedge, with the brushy ends angled out to the other side. Midlands hedging, for example, is always single brushed. Double brushed hedges have pleachers laid in from both sides, with the brushy ends projecting alternately to one side and the other, producing a more symmetrical bushy appearance. Where hedges are not ditched, double brushing serves as an alternate strategy to keep the young shoots from grazing stock, since the shoots growing up in the centre are shielded by a brushy wall on both sides. The true Double Brush type is an extreme version of this method and is explained in detail later in the chapter.

Not all Welsh styles stress the importance of brushing, and no sharp distinction between single and double brush occurs where hedges are unstaked. Some Welsh styles are thin, some bulked out with deadwood cuttings. There is often fierce argument as to the balance required between protecting and possibly smothering the new growth. The Breconshire and some other styles vary depending on the particular situation. Where stock are unlikely to get at the near side of the hedge, as at a stream or road edge, the hedge may be single brushed. Normally however, as one craftsman put it, 'we like the double brushing because it gives the new shoots a bit of peace - they can grow up to the height of the hedge before being exposed to view'.

Some Welsh hedgers use neither stakes nor binders. Others use stakes but no binders. But where one or the other are used they are slightly different from the Midlands types. The stakes are stout, about 3" (75mm) in diameter and pointed at the base with an axe. They are usually driven in at an angle in order to help 'lock' the pleachers into position. Oak is preferred for stakes but usually its expense means that untreated softwood is used instead. Since the stakes are too thick to be trimmed easily with a billhook they are normally sawn off to the required height with a bow saw or power saw to finish. Most hedgers like the stake top to be flush with the top of the hedge, but some prefer to cut it off at right angles to the stake itself because it looks more 'natural', slows rotting by allowing rain to run off, and allows binding (if used) 'to get a better hold of the stakes'. Sawing may not be the best method although it is certainly the easiest. Old craftsmen say that they used to be required to cut stakes off with three cuts of the axe to keep them from rotting as quickly.

TRIMMING STAKES — WALES

sawn flush with hedge top

sawn at right angles to stake

trimmed with axe

When binders are used hazel is preferred as in the Midlands. But the rods used are thicker and less straight, and so are twisted in a simple 2-rod spiral rather than in the 3 or 4-rod pattern of the Midlands.

Secondary features such as the exact type of staking and binding may be a response to climate and weather conditions or may simply reflect the availability of materials. Welsh craftsmen say that Midlands hedges could never stand up to the storms and drifting snows of the upland winter. On the other hand they admire the delicacy of the Midland type's more slender stakes and fine braid of heathering. Those Welsh hedgers who do use stakes often complain that only poor-quality softwood is available. The same holds true for heathering - hazel is in scarce supply on hill farms. Often farm hedges are bound with plain or barbed wire, strained by hand, when no suitable natural material can be found. In this case the wire is twisted around itself in the same way as normal binding.

Interesting features of some Welsh hedges are 'crops' and 'crooks'. Crops are stems left standing in the hedge and cut off at a convenient height to serve as living stakes (p 95). Crooks are small stakes with bent-over tops which, when pushed into the laid hedge, help to hold down the pleachers (p 98). It should be noted that one or the other are most often used when stakes are absent from the hedge. Sometimes this is because the hedge is small, on a high bank, and long stakes are unnecessary. Sometimes it is a way of doing without what is difficult to get. Crops and crooks are handy supports against wind and snow drift and so in some places are used as well as stakes to keep the hedge in place.

A final characteristic of Welsh hedges, at least of those laid in competitions, is the care with which they are trimmed and shaped. Whatever the finished form, most craftsmen 'manicure' the hedge with billhook, grass or gorse hook or even gardener's secateurs until no twig is out of place and the hedge's surface is even and hedgehog-dense. The trimming is done very carefully so as to hide the 'white' on the cut stems. The stems are cut along the grain from the back to the front like this:

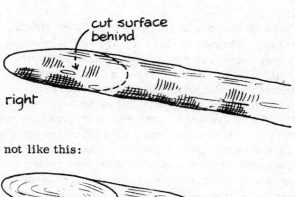

cut surface behind

right

not like this:

wrong

WELSH HEDGING STYLES

Many of the points of variation between different Welsh hedging styles have been mentioned already, since the same features which serve to distinguish Welsh and Midlands hedges often separate Welsh hedges one from another.

The All-Wales Hedging and Ploughing Match (p 112) is the ideal occasion to see the variety which Welsh and border hedging can display. The match is held in a different place each year and is to some extent dominated by local forms, but always there are at least four or five styles represented. Craftsmen and farmers take a keenly critical look at hedges which are laid differently from their own. The arguments pro and con for various styles illuminate the many traditions and requirements within which the Welsh craftsman works.

The summary table which follows groups the dozen or more distinct Welsh styles into four major types. These types have developed in response to particular agricultural and climatic regimes, as well as to general regional differences and traditions. In most cases each type seems well suited to the requirements of its area. When laying a hedge it is always a good idea to see what type of hedge is characteristic for the neighbourhood and to follow along in the same pattern.

In the table, the angles for stakes and pleacher are measured upwards from the bank, taking the bank as 0°. The angles given are averages and are very approximate.

Bank height and hedge height are given as low (L), medium (M) and high (H). These can be taken to be, very approximately, 2'-2'6" (610mm-760mm), 3'-3'6" (910mm-1060mm) and 4' (1220mm) respectively.

Under the 'brushing' column, a dash indicates that brush is not a feature of the hedge or that stakes are not used and therefore the terms 'single' and 'double brushing' do not apply.

Occurance	Angle of stakes	Angle of pleachers	Bank height	Hedge height	Binders	Crooks	Crops	Brushing
Type I: 'Stake and Pleach'								
Monmouthshire	75°–80°	10°–30°	L	M	No	None or single	No	Either
Breconshire	60°–75°	15°–30°	L	M-H	Yes	No	No	Mainly double
Radnorshire (except east)	60°–75° (Similar to Breconshire)	15°–30°	L	M-H	Yes	No	No	Mainly double
Glamorgan uplands	45°–50°	40°–45°	H	M	No	No	No	Either
North Cardiganshire	75°–80°	25°	L-M	M	Yes	No	No	Single
Montgomeryshire	75°–80° (A strong, thick style)	Flat–40°	L	M-H	No	No	Sometimes	Mainly double
Merioneth	75°–80° (A thin style)	30°–40°	L	M-H	No	No	Yes	Mainly single
Denbighshire	75°–80° (Similar to Flintshire)	30°–40°	L	M-H	No	Double	Sometimes [1]	–
Flintshire	75°–80° (A thin style)	30°–40°	L	M-H	No	No	Sometimes	Mainly single
North-east Carmarthenshire	60°–75° (Similar to Breconshire)	15°–30°	L	M-H	Yes	No	No	Mainly double

continued

Type II: 'Crop and Pleach'								
South and east Radnorshire	None used	30°–40°	M	H	Some-times	No	Yes	–
Type III: 'Double Brush'								
Parts of south Montgomery-shire, Breconshire, west Monmouthshire and Glamorgan uplands.	50°–60°	30°–40°	L-M	M	No	No	Some-times	Double
Type IV: 'Flying Hedge'								
Monmouthshire	None used	Flat	H	L	No	Single	Some-times	–
Vale of Glamorgan	None used	Flat	M	L-M	No	Single	Some-times	–
Gower	None used	Nearly flat	M-H	L	No	Yes	No	–
Carmarthenshire (except northeast)	None used	Flat	M	M	No	Yes (along centre)	Yes[2]	–
Pembrokeshire	None used	Flat	M	L	No	Yes	No	–

Notes:

[1] In Denbighshire hedges long double crooks may be used in addition to stakes.
[2] In Carmarthenshire hedges the crops are half the height of the hedge and are placed along the outer edges of the hedge.

'Stake and Pleach'

Of all the Welsh types, the Stake and Pleach hedge most closely resembles the Midlands hedge in form. It is a widespread and diverse type with several distinct subdivisions as shown in the preceeding table. Stake and Pleach hedging in one form or another is found through north and central Wales from Denbigh and Flint south through Merioneth, Montgomeryshire, north Cardigan, west and central Radnor, northeast Carmarthen, parts of Breconshire and Monmouthshire and into the Glamorgan uplands. Hill farms typify these areas. Sheep and cattle are kept in varying proportions depending on elevation, terrain and exposure. Stake and Pleach is used mainly on the mixed farms in the region, while Double Brush is the type most often used on farms which keep sheep exclusively.

The determining characteristics of the type are the use of stakes and the 'weaving' of the pleachers among the stakes. In this sense the Midlands hedge could logically be called a variety of Stake and Pleach, and in fact the type blends into the Midlands form without sharp break in Flint and Cheshire, Shropshire and Herefordshire. In Wales, these hedges usually have the stakes set at an angle to the bank rather than perpendicular, in order to 'lock' the pleachers firmly into place and keep them from springing upwards. Binding may or may not be used. The height and thickness of the finished hedge varies widely from place to place.

Three varieties of Stake and Pleach are illustrated. Some of the less apparent differences between them are listed in the summary table or are described below.

Breconshire

(view from near side)

near or bank side   (section)

3'6"

Monmouthshire — may be single rather than double brushed

single crooks may be used

(view from near side)

(section)

3'-3'6"

Flintshire — may be double rather than single brushed

occasional crops may be used

(view from near side)

(section)

3'6"-4"

CUTTING OUT UNWANTED STEMS (BRECONSHIRE STYLE ONLY)

Craftsmen in the Breconshire style tend to cut out all or virtually all of the unwanted material at the beginning of the day's work, while clearing out rubbish from the hedge bottom and trimming back side growth. Only those stems which it is planned to cut and lay are left standing. Only experts should attempt this. In nearly all cases it seems wiser to trim out in the usual way (p 75) to avoid cutting out material which may be needed after all.

STAKING AND LAYING

In Stake and Pleach hedging, nearly the whole length of each pleacher is woven among the stakes. To do this, keep the staking following on about a yard back of the pleachers. This is in contrast to the Midlands method where only the upper ends of the pleachers are interlaced among the stakes and where more distance is left between the last stake in line and the next pleacher to cut and lay.

Drive the stakes in a straight line down the middle of the hedgerow. Bring pleachers into the line of stakes from both sides as convenient.

This, combined with weaving the pleachers among the stakes, creates a symmetrical hedge, brushy on both sides. Note, though, that in some parts of Monmouthshire and Flintshire the hedges are often single brushed.

Cut off stems which are growing well out of the line of the hedgerow, unless they are essential for pleaching a gap.

Each of the three varieties illustrated differ in the details of staking and laying techniques.

Breconshire

Put the stakes in at about 60º-75º. Angle the stakes against the pleachers in order to lock down the pleachers, as in the diagram.

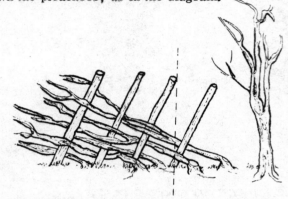

Space the stakes so that the top of one stake is directly over the base of the next stake in line, keeping the bases about 21" (530mm) apart.

Weave each pleacher around each stake in line unless it is too thick near the base to force into this position. This is called 'bowing', and it helps to protect from grazing the shoots which will spring from stools further down the line. Weave in the side branches in the same way, cutting them part way through if necessary to angle them back into the hedge. Try to use as many side branches as possible, cutting off only those which are awkward to weave in.

After completing the staking and laying, bind the top as for the Midlands hedge. Binding, as well as the angled stakes, keeps the pleachers from springing out of position.

Monmouthshire

Place the stakes slightly more upright than in the Breconshire style, about 75º-80º and 24" (610mm) apart.

Weave the pleachers that grow from the near side of the hedge around every pair of stakes. This produces a bowing similar to that of the Brecon-

shire style but less pronounced. The far side requires less attention to appearance and if the hedge is double brushed the pleachers from that side can be woven in as convenient. Weave in side branches in the same way.

Binding is considered unnecessary and most Monmouthshire hedgers do not use it. The angle of the stakes and the weaving serves to hold pleachers in place.

Flintshire

Set the stakes nearly vertically, about 18"-20" (450mm-500mm) apart.

Weave in the pleachers as is convenient. Flintshire hedgers take less trouble to shield the cut stools with other pleachers, in keeping with making a generally 'thin' hedge.

No heathering is used.

USE OF DEADWOOD. FINAL TRIMMING

Breconshire

Stick quite a bit of small deadwood into the hedge during the course of work. This, along with the side branches already woven in, creates a 'bulkier', more massive hedge than would otherwise be possible. Do not use large pleacher-sized stems as deadwood unless you need them to fill a gap. In this case, point the base of each stem, push it into the ground at the same angle as the other pleachers, and weave it in in the same way as the pleachers.

Trim the hedge lightly to make it as uniform as possible and to give it a neat rectangular shape.

Monmouthshire

Use some deadwood brush but not as much as in the Breconshire style.

Trim the hedge so that it is neatly rectangular, although rather thinner than the Breconshire type.

Flintshire

Do not use deadwood except to fill gaps where pleachers are inadequate. To finish the hedge, even out irregularities in the surface with dead brush but do not artificially fill out the hedge's shape. The hedge should be still thinner than the other two styles, and the pleacher stems themselves, not the brush, should form the most obvious part of the barrier.

Carry out final trimming with a billhook alone, not with secateurs. Trim as for a Midlands hedge, without a great deal of fuss.

'Crop and Pleach'

'Crops', 'croppers', 'poles' or 'standards' are stems which are not cut and laid in the usual way but which are instead cut off in an upright position where they emerge from the laid hedge. They act as living stakes, holding the pleachers in place.

Crops are used to some extent throughout central Wales. In Montgomeryshire, Merioneth and Denbighshire some hedgers leave them in when stakes are few and pleachers plentiful. Quite often they use a side branch which is left sticking straight up from a laid pleacher. Instead of lopping it off where it joins the pleacher, they cut it at the right level to make a crop. Some Double Brush hedgers use an occasional supplementary crop, part way out to the side of the hedge, to contain its great width. Carmarthenshire hedgers use half-sized crops in their version of the 'Flying Hedge'. But the 'true' form of Crop and Pleach, resembling Stake and Pleach but dispensing with stakes as much as possible, is restricted to southern and eastern Radnorshire.

CROP AND PLEACH

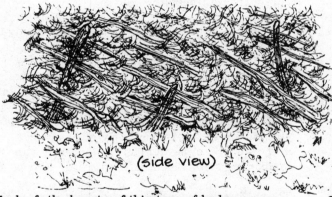

(side view)

Much of the beauty of this type of hedge comes from its proportions and from its rounded top which allows snow to slip off. Its effectiveness comes partly from its crops and partly from the fairly high, double-faced bank. It is perhaps a stronger cattle fence than the Double Brush hedge, but even so there is a danger that cattle will nose under the hedge and lift up the pleachers since there are no stakes or binding.

Crops have several advantages over deadwood stakes:

a   They eliminate the cost of stakes and the labour of preparing them.

b   Being firmly rooted they hold the hedge in place against high winds and heavy snow-drifts where stakes may be knocked about. Cattle pushing on the hedge will not budge crops.

c   They can hold down springy smooth pleachers such as hazel and willow and can contain very big pleachers which might otherwise twist out of position. This, again, is because they are firmly rooted. They work especially well when they are placed in a staggered double line near the outside edges of the hedge rather than up the middle like a row of stakes.

d   Crops sprout where they have been cut off and, to some extent, along the length of their stems. This gives a quick-growing bushy cover to the top of the hedge while other shoots grow more slowly from the stools.

e   Crops do not rot. This is especially helpful where good stakes are unavailable and in exposed wind-swept cold areas where the laid hedge regrows slowly and uncertainly. In these areas all but the best stakes lose their effectiveness before the new growth has fully come up through the pleachers.

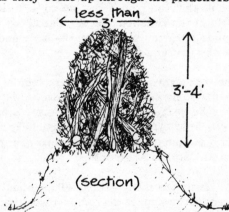

less than 3'

3'-4'

(section)

Crops have three disadvantages which keep most hedgers from using them:

a   They may suppress new basal shoots under their dominant cover. This may cause the hedge to slowly thin out at the bottom or become stunted where the crop has been used.

b   Every crop left is a pleacher lost. This may result in a weak hedge if there are not enough stems for both purposes.

c   Cattle tend to rub on any firm projection in a hedge, such as a crop, and this may cause more damage to the hedge than if the animals ignore it. Cattle may hurt themselves if they slip and fall against a crop.

Crop and Pleach hedgers say that if crops are used carefully and with discrimination, none of these bad effects occur.

CUTTING AND LAYING: USE OF CROPS

Select crops in advance of pleachers so that you force the pleachers between and around the trimmed crops. Choose vigorous, mature but not overly large stems for crops. Crops which are very thick are likely to die and are no stronger than smaller stems. If you do need to use a thick crop, you can encourage it to resprout from the base by cutting out a large notch, about $\frac{1}{4}$ of the way through the stem at the base.

Choose crops which angle out slightly from positions to either side of the centre line of the hedgerow. Avoid crops right along the centre line but also avoid crops far to the edges of the finished hedge.

Cut crops off 'as soon as they've done their work', in other words just where they would emerge from the finished hedge. Crops will usually be 2'-3' (610mm-910mm) tall depending on how they are positioned. Cut them off at an angle so that their ends will blend with the curved profile of the finished hedge. Check for projecting ends after the pleachers are laid, and trim back any that you find.

Do not use crops where there are insufficient stems to make a fairly thick hedge. Instead, where the hedge is thin, use as many pleachers as possible. After laying the pleachers, drive in an occasional stake where crops are missing. Drive the stakes at an angle.

Avoid using too many crops. They should be spaced further apart than stakes would be, although their placement varies depending on what stems are available. It is best to use multiple-stemmed plants where possible, keeping one or two stems as crops and laying as many of the rest as required.

To produce the hedge's rounded profile, lay the larger pleachers lower down when possible. Lay smaller stems to the outside and on top, although if you have additional large pleachers they can be laid on the top along the centre line. This keeps the large pleachers from rolling off to the sides.

If it is difficult to keep the hedge wide enough at the bottom, put in deadwood to fill it out and

protect the cut stools.

Trim up as you work. It helps to trim side branches so that little 'cags' are left on. These can then be used as hooks to hold down other pleachers and branches. This increases the hedge's strength and makes it neater.

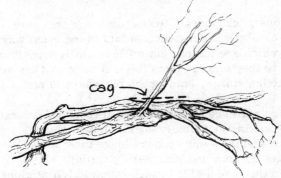

'Double Brush'

The Double Brush hedge carries the thickest of the Stake and Pleach styles to an extreme. Rather than forming the 'typical' type in any region it is found here and there in southern Montgomeryshire, through Breconshire, into the hilly western edge of Monmouthshire and in the Glamorgan uplands. In these areas it represents an alternative to whichever version of Stake and Pleach happens to prevail in the neighbourhood, with some craftsmen adopting Double Brush out of personal preference.

The Double Brush hedge is designed primarily to fence sheep. It is made dense with deadwood, a truly impenetrable barrier until this material rots. New shoots are protected from grazing by the dead brush stuck into the sides. This also keeps the width even and thick from bottom to top. Unlike many hedges the Double Brush is considered sufficiently strong immediately after laying to allow stock into the field and to dispense with temporary wire fences. (See diagram next page.)

This hedge is designed to protect regrowth in the middle. Some critics maintain that the surplus deadwood tends to inhibit this centre growth and that the inevitable result in later years is a 'hollow', weak hedgerow. But craftsmen who work in this style claim that 'nothing can stop new shoots, can it?'

CUTTING, LAYING AND STAKING

The aim is to make a wide hedge, with pleachers coming in from the edges and arching over the centre like a kind of tent. The centre line at ground level is left rather free of pleachers so that regrowth will not be hindered.

DOUBLE BRUSH

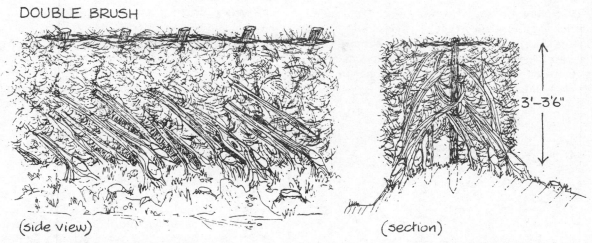

(side view)   (section)

Cut out all large stems which grow from the centre line of the hedge. This frees the centre for regrowth and also avoids the problem of knocking stakes out of line when laying large central pleachers. If there is a lot of centre growth, cut out most of the smaller stems as well.

Cut and lay the stems growing along the outsides of the row. Of course, stems growing from a point far to either side should be cut out since they will not fit in with the general edge of the hedge after laying.

There are two methods if you are working alone. If work is done in pairs, ideal for this type of hedge, adapt method A so that one person works on either side.

Method A

Work mainly from the near side of the hedge. Work along the row, laying in pleachers from both sides as you go, either by reaching through to lay far side pleachers or by crossing over when necessary.

You have the choice of weaving the pleachers between every stake or taking each one outside the first three stakes and tucking in behind the fourth in line. In either case it is best to cut off the ends of the pleachers after about the fifth stake. Try to avoid using very thick pleachers. The top 6"-9" (150mm-225mm) of the hedge should be made up of thinner, brushier material, and this is possible only if the stems are rather small where they are cut off at the fifth stake.

Method B

Cut and lay all pleachers along the near side first. Lay them at an angle of about 30°-40° off the bank so that they cross the stakes roughly at the 18" (450mm) level. The near side pleachers

form the lower part of the hedge. Then cross to the far side and lay the remaining pleachers. Take each one over the top of the adjacent near side pleacher so that they form the top part of the hedge.

It is best to weave the pleachers between each stake when using this method. Again, cut the pleachers off after about the fifth stake.

Drive in stakes at a 50°-60° angle. Space them so that the top of one stake is directly above the bottom of the next one in line.

If the pleachers tend to bow out too much, so that the centre of the hedge is weak, you can leave an occasional crop so as to force the pleachers more tightly toward the centre.

MAINTAINING THE ANGLE OF PLEACHERS. USE OF DEADWOOD

Double Brush uses a great deal of deadwood, including whole stems as well as the usual smaller brush. As you work, cut out any stems which grow at an inconvenient angle, everything that doesn't 'run with the hedge'. This includes major branches which angle up out of line with the pleachers. The idea is to keep the pleachers running all at the same angle and to provide deadwood to fill up any gaps.

Craftsmen in this style say 'If you pleach one in too soon it makes the hedge run flat'. This is easiest to show in a diagram.

Pleacher laid too flat. Put deadwood beneath it to raise to correct angle and fill gap at base.

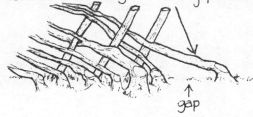

gap

To fill up the space between pleachers and maintain the correct angle, take a deadwood stem, cut off its side branches, point the butt end and drive this into the ground between the live pleachers. Trim off the small end so that it will not project from the finished hedge.

deadwood pleacher

These deadwood 'pleachers' are also used where it is necessary to shield the top of a cut stool on the outside of the hedge and where it is not adequately covered by a real pleacher.

Push smaller deadwood branches and brushy bits into the sides and top of the hedge to build it out into its full, uniform rectangular shape. The hedge should be so dense that you cannot see daylight through it when looking from the sides.

FINISHING

Double Brush hedges, while they have no true binding, have an interlaced top which has a similar purpose in holding down the springy ends of the pleachers. This top is made before the stakes are trimmed.

Take pairs of supple deadwood stems. Force the butt end of each stem into the hedge top between two stakes so that it is held firmly in the hedge. Then bend it over and weave it between each stake in this pattern:

(oblique view)

Insert a new pair of stems where the first pair becomes too thin, after three or four stakes. Tuck the small ends out of sight in the hedge top.

Trim off the stakes level with the top of the hedge. Then go over the whole hedge carefully, trimming it and inserting any final brush so that it presents a uniform, impenetrable and 'clipped' appearance.

'Flying Hedge'

Craftsmen in the Vale of Glamorgan describe their local style as the 'flying' hedge. This apt name is extended here to cover all low hedges with pleachers laid flat or nearly flat along a medium to high double-sided bank. Other common features are the use of crooks rather than stakes and the absence of binding along the top of the hedge.

In the broad sense used here, the Flying Hedge is closely related to the turf hedges of the South West. Interestingly, the Flying Hedge occurs in those parts of Wales which most resemble the South West in climate and topography. It is found from south Cardiganshire across Pembrokeshire and most of Carmarthenshire, through the Gower Peninsula and the Vale of Glamorgan and into Monmouthshire. These are regions of low plateau and rolling hills with sheltered stream valleys, drier and sunnier than the mountainous areas to the north and east. Frosts are rare but southwest gales make shelter important. Farms, mainly mixed, support different breeds of sheep from those in the higher regions. As one Pembrokeshire hedger put it, 'We've all big sheep down here - they won't jump ... but the mountain sheep they'll jump about six feet!' The high banks of the Flying Hedge deter lowland sheep and at the same time provide shelter. The hedge on top improves the barrier but need not be extremely strong on its own. (See diagram next page.)

CUTTING AND LAYING

Lay the pleachers flat or nearly flat, depending on the local style, directly along the top of the bank. Use stems across the full width of the bank, laying into the hedgerow those which are growing out from the edges. But cut away stems which are growing out of the bank sides unless pleachers are in short supply. The finished hedge should be nearly square in cross section, about 1'6" (450mm-610mm) tall and wide.

It helps to deter nosey sheep if you can lay the pleachers so that the hedge is rather wider at the top than at the bottom, with an overhang on each side.

USE OF CROOKS

Crooks or 'ties' are deadwood stems cut so that they hook sharply at the top. They can be single or double.

FLYING HEDGE

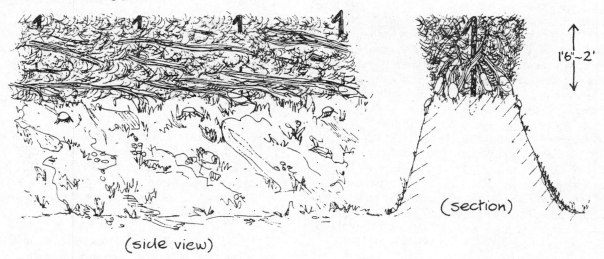

(side view)

(section)

1'6"–2'

SINGLE CROOK DOUBLE CROOK

Length of crook varies with height of hedge

Cutting a crook

Crooks replace stakes in the Flying Hedge. The crooks are put in after a section of hedge has been laid. They are spaced every yard or so along the centre line of the hedge and driven in until tight, about 6" (150mm). They are orientated with the hooked ends running across the lie of the pleachers so that they catch the pleachers and hold them firmly down. Some craftsmen say that, where the wind is strong, single crooks should have their hooks facing into rather than away from the wind so that pleachers are blown tight against the stem of the crook. Others, though, say that it doesn't matter.

It is easiest to find stems to make single crooks, but in some regions double crooks are preferred for strength. Hazel is best if you can find it and cut it in advance. But any suitably shaped branch cut out of the hedgerow can be used. Just be sure that the wood is live when cut.

Crooks are used not only in Flying Hedges. Denbighshire hedgers use double crooks in addition to stakes in their version of Stake and Pleach. The crooks are cut long, so that they can be driven down through the 3'-4' (910mm –

1220mm) high hedge. Stake and Pleach hedgers in Monmouthshire sometimes use single crooks to supplement their stakes in much the same way. A very mixed style is found in Carmarthenshire, where a Flying Hedge of medium height is laid between ½-sized crops which are left near the outer edges of the hedge. Then the centre line is held down with crooks.

South Western Laid Hedges

As has been mentioned already, the great majority of West Country hedges have neven been managed by laying. In fact throughout the South West the bank dominates the hedge if indeed there is much of a living hedge at all. As on Irish 'ditches', gorse is the most useful plant in very exposed situations, particularly near the coast where other species are battered and stunted by the salt wind. Elsewhere briar forms a dense crown on the bank, but in protected locations and increasingly as one moves east, the banks are topped by a luxuriant growth of beech or mixed shrubs. It is in these areas, northeast Devon, western Somerset and Dorset, that laid hedges can be found.

These hedges follow the South Wales 'Flying Hedge' style remarkably closely. Wind rather than snow or cold is the major hazard to hedges in both areas. The sheep are relatively docile and the banks serve to protect the living hedge as much as to form a barrier in themselves.

In north and east Devon and around Exmoor hedging is called 'stooping and laying' or sometimes 'steeping and laying'. First the ditch next to the hedge is dug out. Next the bank is turfed, as described in the next chapter, and finally the hedge is 'stooped' along the top or 'comb' of the bank. The stems are usually laid both ways from the stools, criss-crossing each other to form a dense, rectangular mass. Frequently, a chain saw is used to help cut larger stems, and barbed wire is often stretched along the top afterwards in the place of hazel binding.

'Steeping' is the term used in south Devon. Here it is considered best, if possible, to lay all in one direction, either up the slope or from east to west, ie with the sun. This operation is carried out on both sides of the hedge. The brushy ends of the steepers are angled outward and the height of the steeping is about 1' (300mm). Steepers are held in position either with crooks or by locking the top of each steeper under the stool end of the next steeper in line.

On the Isle of Purbeck in southeastern Dorset a very similar technique is used. The layers are crossed over each other, lying flat on the high bank. The result is a laid hedge about 2' (610mm) high.

We talked to the foreman of an estate, a few miles inland of Purbeck to the northwest, about a roadside hedge which he had laid the year before. He said that very little hedging was now done locally, and that he had done the work mainly to improve the appearance of a plantation entrance off the main road. This hedge was on the flat but if, as usual, it had been on a bank the first step would have been to repair any damage to the bank. The stools in this hedge were spaced far apart, so he had laid the 'plushers' both ways from the stools. He had first laid stems to the left so that they lay flat along the base of the hedge. Next he laid the remaining stems from each stool to the right so that they formed the upper part of the hedge, making a finished height of about 3'3" (985mm). He used no stakes but instead held the plushers by occasional single crooks thrust down along the centre line of the hedge. This was not his usual technique: more frequently he dispenses with crooks and instead uses rather small, flexible sticks wedged into the top of the laid hedge, twisted back over several plushers, and locked into position by short crosspieces. The technique makes a neat job, and the work is 'out of sight like the thatchers' spar'.

Unusually, this hedge was composed mainly of hazel and rhododendron. Most likely it was not purposely planted but was formed from shrubs growing at the edge of the estate woodland. Rhododendron is very brittle when laid. Hazel is normally supple but becomes much more brittle when it grows near the roadside as in this case.

A final type of laid hedge can be found elsewhere in Dorset and in Wiltshire. As reported by Pollard, Hooper and Moore (1974, p194), this type seems rather different from all other styles although, like other South Western hedges, it uses no stakes or 'edders' (binding):

> The laid stems are not in the form of a narrow 'fence' but are spread over about a yard and are roughly hemispherical in section. The purpose of stakes and edders is to keep a laid hedge in position. It may be that the extra weight of material used makes this unnecessary, but we have seen twine tied around these hedges at intervals and this suggests that there is a tendency for them to spring up away from the ground, leaving gaps. The resulting hedge is very dense. As one might expect, this technique is used in sheep grazing areas.

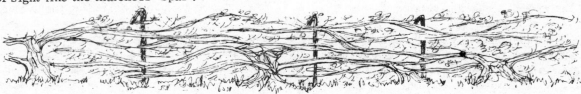

Woodland border hedge — Dorset

10 Banking and Turfing

Turf banks require regular attention if they are to remain effective against livestock. Whether or not they are crowned with live hedges, whether or not the live hedges are cut and laid, banks are subject to their own particular forms of abuse and decay:

a   Strong prevailing winds, although they do no direct harm to a well-maintained bank, cause hedge trees on top to grow towards the lee side. Unless the hedge is laid so as to bring it back along the bank's centre line, the lopsided growth may eventually topple and bring sections of the bank down with it.

b   Soil slump exposes root tips, cutting off nourishment to the shrubs, weakening them and allowing wind to rock them.

c   Trees and to a lesser extent brambles and briars which have rooted in the steep sides of a tall bank tend to dislodge the turf by loosening it.

d   Rabbits and rats can ruin a bank if allowed to burrow into it extensively.

e   Cattle and sheep, being nosey, take advantage of any weak parts of a bank. They paw at the broken turf and scramble up it, accelerating the erosion. Sheep cause additional damage by digging out under the sheltered side of the hedge to escape heavy weather. Where the top growth is not dense, as on many South Western hedges, cattle may clamber to the top simply to find drier grazing.

Worn-out hollows and minor breaks in the turf become obvious when the hedge is given its annual trim. In parts of the South West where the banks become luxuriant with brambles and ivy the bank as well as the hedge may be trimmed, but where conditions are harsh and vegetation slow-growing, or where the sides of the banks are grazed, this trimming is unnecessary and instead the owner should make a point of periodically inspecting the condition of the turf. Where erosion is serious the bank should be fenced off from livestock and repaired as soon as possible. Even where no major repairs are needed, it is best if every year or so fresh earth is cut out along a line at the base of the bank and heaped on top, filling up any hollows which may have developed. In this way the bank is kept at the correct height and the trees growing along it are nourished. If a live hedge is to be laid in the near future and repairs are minor, it is best to wait and carry out the banking and turfing after the hedge has been cleaned out and given its preliminary trim but before it is laid.

Banks and bank maintenance vary from place to place. Banks may have one face or two. They may be a few inches high in north Wales or as much as 6' (2m) or more in the South West. The size and shape of turfs and the number of turfs needed for the job vary as well, along with local names for the turfs and the work. It is worth remembering that in parts of central Wales this work is called 'ditching', the ditch being the raised earth bank. Generally, the higher the bank the less important is any live growth on top and the more developed are banking and turfing, as opposed to hedge laying, techniques. But despite these variations, basic turfing skills are similar everywhere.

In the following pages, preliminary requirements are discussed first, followed by adaptations for group work and the work techniques themselves. How to build a new bank is discussed briefly in the chapter, 'Planting and Early Care'. Not covered in this handbook, though, is the specialised work of building a South Western turf hedge from the ground up. Aside from cutting and handling turf, discussed below, this work is so similar to that of building a stone hedge, which is described in another handbook in this series, 'Dry Stone Walling' (BTCV, 1977).

Protecting the Turfed Bank

Low banks are protected by the measures given to protect the newly laid hedge. Some sheep farmers take no precautions, others use 'byrdn' (p 69) or place brushwood along the face and stake it down. High banks are considered safe from sheep, in fact sheep help preserve the turf by grazing the face and keeping the turf short. This allows rain to soak into the turf and keep it moist, rather than run off as it would from long, shaggy grass.

Cattle are a different matter. Pawing and leaping bullocks menace even the highest banks. West Country hedges of both turf and stone used to be left half built to settle and even now are considered 'tender' until new vegetation starts to grow on them. Letting cattle get at a new hedge during this period is asking that it be torn down. Mended gaps in an otherwise stable bank can be blocked off with a few cut thorn bushes or fenced with a single line of barbed wire, and some farmers trust to watchfulness and frequent repairs to save the cost of fencing. But where the expense can be met, most farmers recommend a permanent fence (p 52).

Weather Precautions

Banking and turfing can be carried out in most areas at any season, although it is more comfortable to work in cool weather. A few precautions should be kept in mind:

a   Avoid working in an exposed place in a high wind. Much of the dirt needed for backing the turfs will blow into your eyes or over the fields.

b   Do not work in a downpour or after heavy rains when the bank is sodden. You will only churn the turfs into mud.

c   High banks take a few days to stabilise when newly turfed. Avoid major repairs if a big storm is due: heavy rains may loosen and wash out all your work.

d   Under certain conditions turf may dry out before it has fully knitted into the earth backing. Large overhanging trees shield turf from rainfall and may draw moisture out of the bank. It is best not to turf here while the tree is in leaf. Where rainfall is light or moderate or where the bank is exposed to drying winds, turfing is best done in the autumn to avoid both dry spells and frost, although near the sea, where mist keeps the windward side of a bank moist, turfing can be done any time over the autumn or winter. It may be that in these areas it is the leeward side which is in danger of dessication, in which case this side should be done at the back end of the year.

Group Work

Turfing in many ways is like hedge laying. The satisfactions come in seeing one's own job well done. As in hedge laying, the opportunities for direct cooperation between workers are limited. In most cases it is best to each take a section of the bank and work at it alone. The length appropriate depends on the bank's height and the amount of work to be done.

If the bank is low and has a hedge which is to be laid immediately afterwards, it is best for the group to concentrate on the length which it is planned to lay that same day. Since turfing is faster than hedging, on low banks, extra volunteers can start cutting and laying the hedge once the turfers have progressed a safe distance along each stretch. Billhooks and mattocks don't mix!

High banks are much more difficult, especially for beginners, so each worker should take a section a few yards long. In turf hedging competitions, where the entire face is torn down and rebuilt, juniors and novices are usually assigned 9' (2.8m) lengths and older and more experienced competitors 12' (3.7m). The time limit is three hours and competitors are often hard pressed to finish. These lengths are about right for a full work day at a reasonable pace.

On high banks lifting and placing the turfs is tiring work, so it may be best if volunteers work in pairs. One person cuts and lifts the turfs while the other prepares the backing, helps take the turf off the shovel without dropping it and tamps it into position. Before the cutter/lifter becomes exhausted they should switch positions. In commercial work, of course, it is expected that a craftsman should be able to cut and throw a turf onto the highest bank 'without the assistance of help or hand'.

Where the bank has two faces, both of which need repair, half the group can work on one side and half on the other. Don't try this, though, on very high banks which might collapse if both faces are torn apart at once.

Banking and Turfing Procedures

Carry out only the work required. Serious breaks and eroded areas should always be repaired as soon as possible. Welsh banks are normally returfed along their length as a part of the hedge laying operation. By contrast, the only work normally done along the whole length of high West Country banks is that every year or two soil is cut out at the base and placed along the top. This nourishes the plants growing there and makes good any slumping of the earth at the base. Only gaps and damaged turf are repaired otherwise, except in competition work when the whole face is torn down and rebuilt.

If the bank has just one face, turf on this side only. If a high, double-faced bank needs extensive rebuilding the repairs should be completed on one side before the other side is touched. This helps keep it stable during work.

The following procedure covers the complete sequence for major repairs. Ordinary gapping work is done in the same way except that you needn't bother with setting out the line or cutting such regular turfs. Be sure even so that you back the turfs with earth fill, break the joints between courses, maintain the correct batter and keep the work well tamped.

Note that if the hedge is to be laid after turfing, the initial trimming and cleaning out of undergrowth should be done before the turfing work commences.

1   Prepare the bank for returfing by cleaning out gaps and eroded areas (see below).

2   Peg out a string along the base of the bank to mark the position of the first cut. The line should 'follow the natural run of the hedge', conforming to gradual curves and bulges but cutting off small irregularities caused by erosion or slippage. Where the run is straight a string makes for the neatest job, but where there are subtle changes of direction expert craftsmen prefer to judge the line by eye in order to avoid an 'engineered' look.

3   Make a series of downward cuts with spade or shovel along the line to mark its position on the ground. Then remove the string.

Welsh hedgers sometimes reuse the string, moving it to the top of the bank to measure where they should finish turfing. They may raise it once again to mark the height to which the hedge should be laid particularly in competition work.

4   Cut out and place the first course of turfs (see below).

5   Place additional courses as required. Break the joints between turfs in alternate courses, as in a brick wall.

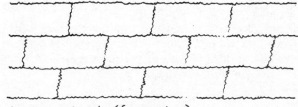

turfs on bank (face view)

Keep the backing well filled and tamped. Keep the courses running level and, in West Country turfing, try to make all courses of the same thickness.

Set each course very slightly back from the course below. This, plus the inward tilt of each turf, ensures that rain runs into rather than drains off the bank. The opposite effect, known in Devon as 'thatching' or 'datching', causes the upper part of each turf to dry out and become powdery.

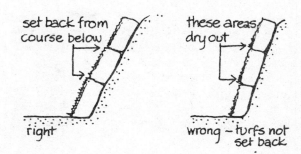

set back from course below

right

these areas dry out

wrong – turfs not set back

Maintain the proper batter in each course of turfs (see below).

6   Bring the turf up to the top or 'comb' of the bank. The exact height relative to the comb varies, as diagrammed below. In any case finish off with loose, good soil along the top and around the bases of the hedge plants.

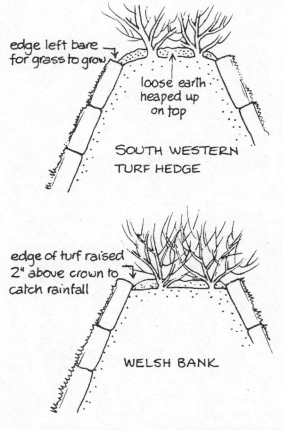

edge left bare for grass to grow

loose earth heaped up on top

SOUTH WESTERN TURF HEDGE

edge of turf raised 2" above crown to catch rainfall

WELSH BANK

7   Clean up the work area after finishing the bank. Move any unwanted dislodged rocks out of the way of beasts and machines. Pull excess soil back over the area where turfs were cut and use the digger or mattock to break down the sharp edge between the cutting and the uncut field. This helps the scars heal over quickly.

8   Cut and lay the hedge, if necessary (see the preceding chapter).

PREPARING THE BANK

Use the digger or mattock to pull out loose sods and earth in order to expose the firm fill at the base and centre of the bank. Cut away ragged edges and overhanging turf and make sure that the cleaned-up area slopes slightly inward as well as widens out from bottom to top. This allows the repair work to key into the existing bank.

BANK REPAIRS

Face view

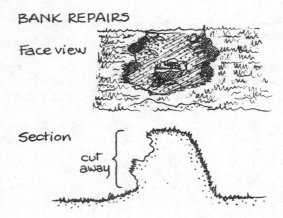

Section

Clear out shrubs growing in the bank side and cut off trees which grow from the side except where they are required for hedge laying.

Keep the loose earth piled near the base of the bank, to be reused as backing for the new turfs, but leave room right at the base to cut your first course of turfs. In West Country turf hedging competitions, where the side of the bank is cut back to perpendicular and down as far as the 'foundations', ie the level of the field, a great deal of the bank ends up around the craftsmen's feet. Many competitors bring polythene sacks so that they can shovel fine soil into the sacks as they tear down the bank. They then heave the sacks up to the crown or 'comb' of the bank to get them out of the way and to make sure that they have good soil at the end for finishing off the top.

Another competition innovation which makes for neater work is to lay down matting or old boards where you plan to dig out the new turfs, before beginning to tear down the bank. This protects the turf from trampling; as you work you can shift the matting or boards back to areas which you will cut later.

CUTTING AND PLACING TURFS

The diagram shows the usual position of the string and the first course of turfs cut from the field. Cut succeeding courses progressively

further away from the bank. Where the field is patchy and bare, turfs must be cut wherever the grass is best, but if possible keep the digging near to the bank for efficiency and neatness. Large stones in the turf can be set aside or used to help fill in deep hollows in the bank.

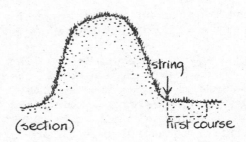

First course cutting methods

Method A. Cut out a notch using the line already cut as the back of the notch (step 3, above). Spread the soil from the notch on the top of the bank and wherever the face needs filling out, turning the grass green side down. Then cut out the first course of turfs using this notch as a backing line.

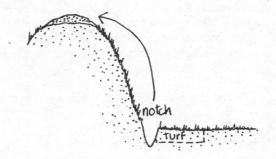

Method B. Cut out the first course of turfs directly, using the guideline as the back cut. Place the turfs in position against the face of the bank as you cut them. Then dig out the trench where the turfs were, to get more soil as backing for the turfs or for the bank top.

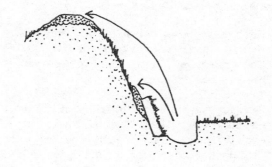

Whichever method you use, pack the loose soil onto the bank face where gulleys and sags need filling in and along the top to even out hollows and dips. Do not pile the earth up around the stems of the hedge trees; when these are cut and laid the pleacher stools should not be covered with earth.

Fill any hollows and dips along the top

Backing and packing the turfs

Wherever the bank face has been torn down, either to remove poor old turf or to clean out a gap, the proper backing for new turfs must be provided <u>before</u> placing the turfs. Use earth cleaned out of the gap or else dug from the trench left by the removed turfs. Keep the backing well filled and somewhat above each course of turfs as it is placed. Tamp the earth fill with spade or digger so that it is well firmed before the turfs are placed against it. This is how the work should proceed:

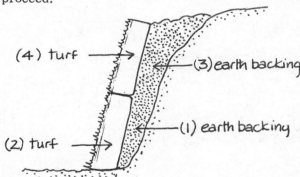

(4) turf
(3) earth backing
(1) earth backing
(2) turf

Where only a little earth is needed behind the turfs, as when adjusting the batter (see below), you can place each turf first, shovel in the required amount of fill behind it and then pack both turf and fill at the same time.

Welsh workers use the flat of the spade or the sole of the foot to tamp the turfs. In the West Country the digger is used instead - the method is described on page 36 . In competitions, craftsmen tamp turfs at the top and sides only, to avoid smearing the faces. This is important in any case to knit each turf to the one beside it, eliminating as far as possible the visible joints. Turfs which are cut on the slant knit in more easily than turfs with squared edges.

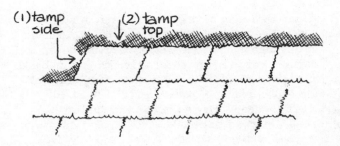

(1) tamp side
(2) tamp top

You can keep the turf steady and in one piece if you place your foot against its face while tamping it.

Set each turf so that it tilts inward slightly. This helps rain to run into the bank and also keeps the turf from falling outward as the bank settles.

right
tilt turf inward slightly
wrong

Direction of work

Cut the turfs working either from right to left or from left to right as convenient. Here is how to cut each turf if you are working from right to left:

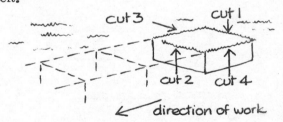

cut 3
cut 1
cut 2
cut 4
direction of work

Cut out succeeding courses of turfs in this way, if working from right to left:

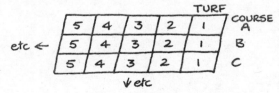

					TURF COURSE
5	4	3	2	1	A
5	4	3	2	1	B
5	4	3	2	1	C

etc ←

↓ etc

Size and shape of turfs

Turfs can be cut in various shapes and sizes, depending on soil conditions and on local tradition. Bigger turfs can be cut in heavy soil, although it is hard to handle turfs much over 1' (300mm) square. Big turfs make the work go faster, but on a high bank of many courses they tend to knit together less well than do smaller turfs. Light soil requires smaller, thinner turfs, but it is important to get at least 4" (100mm) of soil under the grass or else the turfs tend to 'buckle at the knees' under the weight of turfs above. Soil depth is very important for strength in high banks where you should aim for turfs the full depth of the shovel blade, if possible, or at least 6" (150mm) deep. Dry soils compact better than wet soils which get muddy and slippery so try to do your turfing when the fields are fairly dry.

The variety of turf shapes and the ways in which they are placed on the bank are best shown by examples. The diagrams indicate the typical number of courses needed in each case, but be prepared to add or subtract courses for banks of varying heights. Bank heights are average. In all cases the field at the base of the bank is smoothed over after turfing is finished.

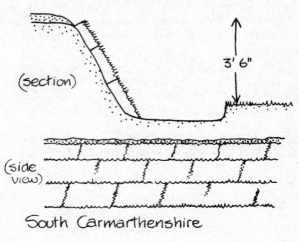

South Carmarthenshire

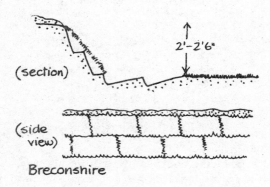

Monmouthshire, Radnorshire

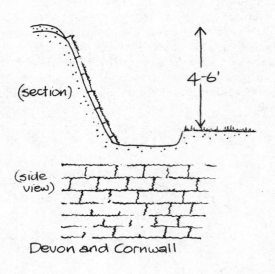

Devon and Cornwall

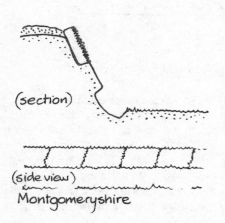

Breconshire

Montgomeryshire

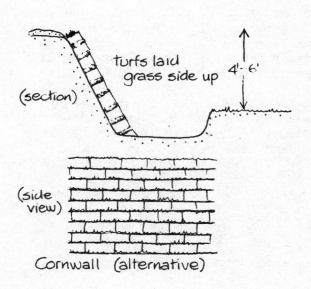

Cornwall (alternative)

Notice in the Montgomeryshire example that the turfs are dug from the base of the bank face and placed on a shelf cut so that their tops are at the proper height. This means that the bank is steepened against the effects of soil slump. Only one course of large turfs is normally used in this style.

The alternative Cornish example shows the turfs turned so that the grass is buried. This method is slower than the usual West Country style but is useful when filling in deep hollows on the bank face or when working with mucky and crumbly turfs which lose their shape and flop off the shovel onto their faces.

Another West Country variation, not shown, is to lay the foundation layer grassy side up in order to give a wider base, and then to place succeeding layers face outward as usual.

BATTER

The 'batter' of a bank is the pitch at which its face slopes. This usually is expressed as a ratio. For example, a batter of 1:3 means that the bank slopes inward one unit in every three vertical units. A 6' (1830mm) bank of 1:3 batter on each face is 4' (1220mm) narrower at the top than at the bottom.

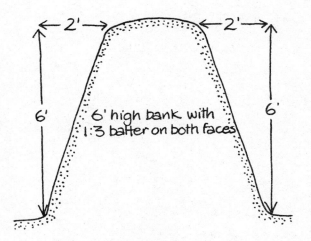

On high West Country banks the batter for new work is set by building to a special wooden or metal pattern. For repair work it is easier to maintain the batter by eye, judging from the existing bank, than to try to measure it exactly. West Country turf hedges usually vary between 1:3 and 1:6. A Devon hedge 6' (1830mm) high normally has a batter of 1'6"-2' (450-610mm) on each face, depending on the shape of the land and the orientation of the face. East or north faces normally require a more gradual batter to counteract the limited rainfall to these faces. Welsh banks vary even more than do those in the South West, perhaps because the batter is less important on lower banks. In every case you should be prepared to adjust to the requirements of individual cases.

Low banks of only a course or two should be steepened during repair in order to correct the usual slumping of the soil. Restore a batter of between 1:2 and 1:6 to these banks by adding more earth fill behind the top than the bottom of each turf.

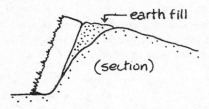

In the Montgomeryshire style the fill is taken from the ledge cut out to hold the turfs, as well as from the trench from which the turfs are cut, and is placed on the bank first followed by the turfs.

Tall banks, if built with a straight batter, tend to 'belly out' as they settle, particularly if the land is higher on one side of the bank than the other. This is why, although some Cornish banks are built straight, most West Country banks are built about 2" (50mm) concave. During settling the concave face straightens or remains very

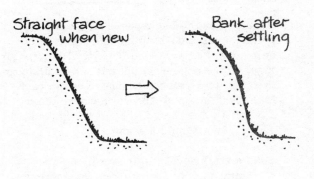

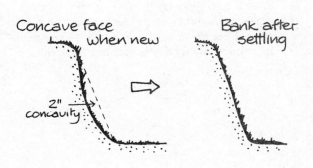

slightly concave. The 2" concavity should be restored during repair so that, as it settles, the repaired area comes to resemble the rest of the bank. Another advantage of a slightly concave face is that it deflects air currents upwards, giving better shelter on the leeward side.

On a high bank the evenness of the batter can be checked with a plumbline as you work. The idea is to distribute the slope evenly through all the courses. If the batter is concave this concavity should also be evenly distributed: lower courses tilted back more, upper courses nearly vertical. The concave batter of a typical turf hedge approximates the usual curve of a Devon shovel stick. By holding the shovel against the hedge, blade up, you can see how you are doing.

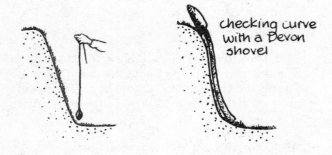

checking curve with a Devon shovel

TESTS FOR FIRMNESS

If you want to judge your own work the way it would be in West Country competition, try these tests for firmness:

a   Climb up on the bank where it is old and solid. Then side-step along it, carefully going over the newly-built part. Do not step right on the edge - the idea is not to dislodge turfs but to sense the firmness of the packing. Gently hop up and down where the new earth fill joins the solid heart of the bank. The packing should not give.

b   Take a stick about 2' (610mm) long and ¼" (6mm) in diameter. From ground level, go over some of the joints between turf blocks, seeing how easy or hard it is to push the stick through the earth packing. The stick should not go in easily - if it does the packing is so soft that it is liable to subside.

Hedgerow Surveys

MIXED HEDGE SURVEY FORM

(This sample form is based on one developed by the Cambridgeshire and Isle of Ely Naturalists' Trust.)

Parish(es):   Locality:[2]

Grid reference:[1] __ __ / __ __ __ __ __ __

Date of survey:

Total length of hedge (yards):

Managed by:	Adjacent land use:	Significance of hedge:
___ clipping	___ pasture ___ stream	___ parish boundary
___ layering	___ field ___ road	___ county boundary
___ not managed	___ garden	___ old lane
___ other	___ other	___ other
(specify):	(specify):	(specify):

Historical reference:[3]

Further comments:[4]

Dominant species:[5]

30 yard lengths:[6]

	1	2	3	4	5
Ash	_	_	_	_	_
Beech	_	_	_	_	_
Blackthorn	_	_	_	_	_
Crab apple	_	_	_	_	_
Dog rose	_	_	_	_	_
Dogwood	_	_	_	_	_
Elder	_	_	_	_	_
Elm	_	_	_	_	_
Maple	_	_	_	_	_
Guelder rose	_	_	_	_	_
Hawthorn	_	_	_	_	_
Hazel	_	_	_	_	_
Privet	_	_	_	_	_
Plum	_	_	_	_	_
Spindle	_	_	_	_	_
Sycamore	_	_	_	_	_
Wayfaring tree	_	_	_	_	_
Willow	_	_	_	_	_
_____	_	_	_	_	_
_____	_	_	_	_	_
Species total	_	_	.	_	_

Map:[7]

Notes on ground flora:[6]

Recorder's name and address:

Notes:
[1] Ordnance Survey map reference: The first two spaces are for the 100km square.
[2] Give as much information as possible.
[3] Published or manuscript material. Give title, author and page number of books; catalogue number and source of manuscripts etc.
[4] Kind and number of large and small trees; indications of natural or planted origin; any immediate dangers to hedge; evidence of wildlife value, etc.
[5] The kind of tree or shrub which appears to be most abundant in the hedge.
[6] See survey procedure description (next page)
[7] Draw a sketch map showing exactly where the hedge begins and ends. Include enough surrounding detail so that another person can locate the hedge on an OS map.

The form on the preceding page is based on one used by the Cambridgeshire and Isle of Ely Naturalists' Trust Ltd, for a survey carried out during 1972 and 1973. The survey was to find hedges which are species-rich, have a varied ground flora or other wildlife importance (particularly substantial hedges in otherwise bare landscapes) or are of historical interest. Hedges are classified into pure thorn hedges, mainly recent, elm hedges indicating old enclosures, 'mild' mixed hedges of Tudor vintage, and true mixed hedges with many shrub species intermingled along their entire length. Other indicators of relative conservation value are the hedge's relationship to its surroundings, its health and continuity and the particular need for hedge protection in certain parts of the county.

During the survey, over 270 hedges were recorded and many more examined. From these a list of the most important hedges was drawn up, giving a base from which decisions about conservation management could be taken.

HOW TO DO A HEDGE DATING SURVEY

Hedgerow surveys are open to all, since the only requirement is the ability to recognise hedgerow shrubs. Make sure you have the landowner's permission before conducting any work on private land. See sample form on preceding page.

Procedure

1   Try to find at least twelve hedges in the study area, preferably with a wide age variation, which can be dated by documents.

2   Record the shrubs in these hedges to establish the exact age-species relationship which is likely to hold in your area.

3   Take 30 yard sections for samples. Choose these randomly, trying to avoid biased selection. Remember that the end of a hedge may be atypical, especially if it adjoins a wood or spinney. The simplest way is to pace out a set distance from where you approach the hedge, for example, ten paces, and then record the next 30 yards of hedge.

4   Record only one side of the hedge. Include trees and established shrubs which are clearly part of the hedge. Ignore seedlings. Also exclude climbers and stragglers such as honeysuckle and bramble. Note certain shrubs which indicate 'woodland relic' hedges, eg hazel, spindle, field maple and dogwood. Hawthorn and elm are assumed

to be planted. Frequent colonisers of planted hedges are blackthorn, rose, ash and elder. Certain herbaceous plants also indicate a woodland origin. In Huntingdon these include dog's mercury, bluebell, primrose, wood anemone, wood spurge, wood melick, crested cow wheat and yellow archangel. Other areas may have a rather different 'relic' flora. Do not count herbaceous species for dating purposes.

5   The more lengths of hedge recorded the better, although often only three or four will be possible. Subsequent 30 yard lengths can be marked off continuing along the hedge from the first.

Conservation and the Volunteer Worker

The British Trust for Conservation Volunteers aims to promote the use of volunteers on conservation tasks. In addition to organizing work projects it is able, through its affiliation and group schemes, to offer advice and help with insurance cover, tool purchase and practical technical training.

To ensure the success of any conservation task it is important that the requesting person or agency, the volunteer and the leader all understand their particular responsibilities and roles. All voluntary work should be undertaken in the spirit of the Universal Charter of Volunteer Service, drawn up by the UNESCO Co-ordinating Committee for International Voluntary Service. Three of its most important points are:

1   'The work to be done should be a real need in its proper context and be directly related to a broad framework of development'. In terms of conservation, this means that tasks should be undertaken as integral parts of site management plans, not as isolated exercises. Work should never be undertaken solely for the benefit of the volunteer. Necessary follow-up work after tasks should be planned beforehand to ensure that volunteer effort is not wasted.

2   'The task should be a suitable assignment for a volunteer.' Volunteers cannot successfully tackle all types of work and they should not be used where there is a risk of serious accident or injury, where a financial profit will be made from their labours, where the job is so large that their efforts will have little overall effect, where the skills required are beyond their capabilities so that a bad job results and they become dispirited, or where machines can do the same job more efficiently and for a lower cost.

3   'Voluntary service should not replace paid local labour.' It should complement such work, not supplement it. Employers should make sure in advance that the position of volunteers and paid workers is clear with respect to any relevant labour unions. Further advice may be found in 'Guidelines for the relationships between volunteers and paid non-professional workers', published by the Volunteer Centre, 29 Lower King's Road, Berkhamstead, Hertfordshire HP4 2AB.

Volunteers are rarely 'free labour'. Someone has to pay for transport, materials, tools, insurance, refreshments and any accommodation charges. Before each party makes a commitment to a project it should be clear who is to pay for what. While volunteers may willingly fund their own work, 'user bodies' should be prepared to contribute and should not assume that all volunteers, who are already giving their time and effort, will be able to meet other expenses out of their own pockets. Several grant-aiding bodies may help pay the cost of environmental and conservation projects, notably the Nature Conservancy Council, the World Wildlife Fund and the Countryside Commissions. Details may be found in 'A guide to grants by the Department of the Environment and associated bodies for which voluntary organizations may be eligible', available from the Department of the Environment, Room C15/11, 2 Marsham Street, London SW1P 3EB.

It is important that volunteer workers be covered by some sort of public liability insurance for any damage or injury they may cause to property or to the public. Cover up to £250,000 is recommended. Additional insurance to compensate the volunteer for injury to him- or herself or to other volunteers on task should also be considered.

The volunteer group organizer should visit the work site well before the task, to check that the project is suitable and that volunteers will not be exploited, and to plan the best size of working party and the proper tools and equipment. Volunteers should be advised in advance on suitable clothing for the expected conditions. They should be physically fit and come prepared for work and they should genuinely want to volunteer - those 'press-ganged' into service are likely to work poorly, may do more harm than good and may be put off a good cause for life! Young volunteers need more supervision and are best suited to less strenuous jobs, and it is recommended that where they are involved the task should emphasize education. Note that the Agriculture (Avoidance of Accidents to Children) Regulations, 1958, legally restrict the riding on and driving of agricultural machines, vehicles or implements by children under 13 years.

Volunteer group organizers and 'user bodies' both should keep records of the work undertaken: the date of the project, jobs done, techniques used, number of volunteers and details of any notable events including accidents, unusual 'finds', publicity etc. Such information makes it easier to handle problems or queries which may arise after the task. It also provides a background on the task site for future visits, supplies practical data by which the site management plan can be evaluated and allows an assessment to be made of the volunteer effort.

Associations, Competitions, Courses and Grants

ASSOCIATIONS AND COMPETITIONS

The National Hedge Laying Society was formed in 1978 with the following aims:

a to encourage the craft of hedge laying and keep the local styles in existence

b to train young people in the craft

c to encourage landowners to manage hedges by laying

d to improve hedge laying standards.

The society issues a newsletter and basic instruction leaflets, offers to find hedge layers for clients, and compiles annually a list of instructors. In 1983, 38 instructors were listed in England and Wales, giving a clear indication that hedge laying is not a dying art!

The address of the NHLS is NFYFC Centre, National Agricultural Centre, Kenilworth, Warwickshire CV8 2LG.

The NHLS also runs the National Hedge Laying Championships, and assists other groups wishing to run hedge laying events. The 6th National Hedge Laying Championships, in October 1984, were held as part of the Farmers Weekly 'Field Boundaries Event', which included demonstrations of hedging, fencing and walling. The National Hedge Laying Championships are held annually on the last weekend in October. For details contact the NHLS at the address given above.

Other hedge laying competitions are held in various parts of the country, organised mainly by local agricultural, ploughing or hedging societies. One of the earliest events each year in the Midlands is the Forest of Arden Agricultural Society match, which takes place on the third Thursday in September. Their Honorary Secretary is Mr R A Snow, Trustee Savings Bank, 2 Hawkhurst Road, Maypole, Birmingham B14 5HS. Some hunts still run competitions, though fewer than formerly.

Local Welsh competitions are held mainly in September and October, or in March through to May, avoiding harsh mid-winter weather. The All Wales Ploughing and Hedging Match is held in a different location each year, to encourage participation from each part of the country in turn. For information on this and other Welsh events, contact the Secretary, The Royal Welsh Agricultural Show, Llanelwed, Builth Wells, Powys.

In the South West, turf and stone hedging replaces hedge laying. The big competition is the West of England Ploughing and Hedging Championship, held in mid autumn. For details contact Mr J Alsey, County Organiser, YFC Office, Agriculture House, Truro, Cornwall. A particularly good Young Farmers' turf hedging competition is held by the South Devon YFC around the end of November. For details contact Mr J Connabeer, Hood Barton, Dartington, Totnes, Devon.

COURSES AND EXAMINATIONS

The National Hedge Laying Society compiler an annual list of courses in hedge laying run by agricultural colleges, mostly open to anyone interested. In 1983-84 for example, the following colleges ran short courses in hedge laying:

Derbyshire College of Agriculture, Broomfield, Morley, Derby.

Warwickshire College of Agriculture, Moreton Hall, Moreton Morrell, Warwickshire.

North Oxfordshire Technical College, Agricultural Section, 46a Mewburn Road, Banbury, Oxfordshire OX16 9NZ.

Turf hedging courses are organised by Bicton College of Agriculture, East Budleigh, Budleigh Salterton, Devon EX9 7BY.

The aim of the courses is usually to prepare and examine students according to the hedge laying or turf hedging tests set by the National Proficiency Tests Council. Standards set by this organisation ensure that those who pass are fully qualified to do skilled farm hedging work. The basis for examination is similar to that used in competitions, so that taking a course is useful preparation for the novice competitor. Copies of tests and guide notes can be obtained from The National Proficiency Tests Council, c/o YFC Centre, National Agricultural Centre, Kenilworth, Warwickshire CV8 2LG.

Courses run by the Agricultural Training Board are only open to people employed in agriculture or horticulture. However, the local ATB office (address in local telephone directory) may be able to help with finding instructors for groups wishing to organise their own training courses.

The British Trust for Conservation Volunteers runs training courses on a variety of practical conservation management topics, including hedging. For more information contact your regional office or the headquarters of the BTCV (addresses on page 114).

GRANTS

The Countryside Commission can offer a grant of up to 50% for the restoration of hedges and hedge-banks which are 'visually important', and are part of proposals for a farm conservation plan. It is not able to grant aid subsequent maintenance. Grants can be given to farmers, landowners, local authorities, parish councils and voluntary organisations, and under certain circumstances some public bodies. Further details are given in CCP171 'Conservation grants for farmers and landowners' and CCP172 'Conservation grants for local authorities, public bodies and voluntary organisations', available from the Countryside Commission.

The Ministry of Agriculture, Fisheries and Food can offer a grant, either under the Agriculture and Horticulture Development Scheme (for approved development plans), or the Agriculture and Horti-culture Grant Scheme (for individual items of capital expenditure). Grants can be offered for the provision, replacement or improvement of hedges and associated gates. Under the Agri-culture and Horticulture Development Scheme, the standard rate of grant is 32.5%, which increases to 60% in Less Favoured Areas (mainly upland). Under the Agriculture and Horticulture Grant Scheme, the standard rate of grant is 20%, or 60% in Less Favoured Areas. MAFF grants are available to most farm and horticultural holdings, provided that they are run as commercial businesses. More details can be obtained from your local MAFF office.

The Countryside Commission Grant Aid for Special Projects is a scheme to aid the further development of countryside conservation work by the National Federation of Young Farmers' Clubs, the National Hedge Laying Society and the Dry Stone Walling Association. The scheme is aimed to help local groups carry out particular conservation schemes, to run courses and competitions, and to organise publicity events. The scheme is open to members of the NHLS, the DSWA and societies affiliated to the NFYFC. Further details can be obtained from the NFYFC (address on page 115). The NFYFC provide an administrative service for the NHLS and the DSWA, who can be contacted at the same address.

Conservation and Amenity Organizations

The Arboricultural Association
Ampfield House Romsey Hants
0794 68717

Botanical Society of the British Isles
c/o Department of Botany,
British Museum (Natural History)
Cromwell Road London SW7

British Association of Nature Conservationists
Rectory Farm Stanton St John,
Oxford OX9 1HF

British Ecological Society
Burlington House Piccadilly London
W1V 0LQ

British Trust for Conservation Volunteers
Head Office: 36 St Mary's Street,
Wallingford Oxfordshire OX10 0EU
0491 39766

North East: Springwell Conservation Centre
Springwell Road, Wrekenton, Gateshead
Tyne and Wear NE9 7AD   091 4820111

North West: 40 Cannon Street, Preston,
Lancs PR1 3NT   0772 50286

Yorkshire and Humberside: Conservation
Volunteers Training Centre Balby Road,
Doncaster DH4 0RH   0302 859522

East Midlands: Conservation Volunteers
Training Centre Old Village School
Chestnut Grove Burton Joyce, Nottingham
NG14 5DZ   060231 3316

West Midlands: Conservation Centre,
Firsby Road Quinton, Birmingham B32 2QT
021 426 5588

Wales: The Conservation Centre, Forest
Farm Road Whitchurch Cardiff CF4 7JH
0222 626660

East Anglia: Animal House, Bayfordbury
Estate, Hertford, Herts SG13 8LD
0992 53067

South West: The Old Estate Yard, Newton
St Loe, Bath Avon BA2 9BR
02217 2856

London: The London Ecology Centre,
80 York Way London N1 9AG
01 278 4293/4/5

South: Hatchlands, East Clandon, Guildford,
Surrey GU4 7RT   0483 223294

Northern Ireland: The Pavilion, Cherryvale
Park, Ravenhill Road, Belfast BT6 0BZ
0232 645169

British Trust for Ornithology
Beech Grove, Tring, Hertfordshire HP23 5NR
044282 3461

Conservation Society
12a Guildford Street, Chertsey, Surrey
KT16 9BQ   093 28 60975

Council for Environmental Conservation
Zoological Gardens, Regents Park, London
NW1   01 722 7111

Council for Environmental Education
School of Education, University of Reading.
London Road Reading, Berkshire
RG1 5AQ   0734 875234

Council for the Protection of Rural England
4 Hobart Place London SW1W 0HY
01 235 9481

Council for the Protection of Rural Wales
31 High Street, Welshpool, Powys SY21 7JP
0938 2525

Country Landowners Association
16 Belgrave Square London SW1X 8PQ
01 235 0511

Countryside Commission
John Dower House, Crescent Place.
Cheltenham Gloucestershire GL50 3RA
0242 521381

Countryside Commission for Scotland
Battleby, Redgorton. Perthshire PH1 3EW
0738 27921

Dartington Institute
Central Office, Shinners Bridge, Dartington,
Totnes, Devon PQ9 6JE   0803 862271

Dry Stone Walling Assocation
NFYFC, National Agricultural Centre,
Kenilworth, Warwickshire CV8 2LG
0203 56131

Farming and Wildlife Advisory Group
The Lodge Sandy, Bedfordshire SG19 2DL
0767 80551

Field Studies Council
62 Wilson Street, London EC2A 2BU
01 247 4651

Forestry Commission
231 Corstorphine Road, Edinburgh EH12 7AT
031 334 0303

Friends of the Earth
377 City Road London EC1V 1NA
01 837 0731

The Game Conservancy
Burgate Manor, Fordingbridge, Hampshire
SP6 1EF   0425 52381

Institute of Terrestrial Ecology
68 Hills Road, Cambridge CB2 1LA
0223 69745

International Union for the Conservation of
Nature and Natural Resources
1196 Gland, Switzerland

Landscape Institute
12 Carlton House Terrace, London SW1Y 5AH
01 839 4044

Ministry of Development, Government of Northern
Ireland - Conservation Branch
Parliament Buildings, Stormont, Belfast
BT4 3SS

National Association for Environmental Education
Mr P D Neal, General Secretary, 20 Knighton
Drive, Four Oaks, Sutton Coldfield,
West Midlands B74 4QP

National Farmers Union
Agriculture House, 25-31 Knightsbridge,
London SW1X 7NJ   01 235 5077

National Farmers Union of Scotland
17 Grosvenor Crescent, Edinburgh EH12 5EN
031 337 4333

National Federation of Young Farmers Clubs
National Agricultural Centre, Kenilworth,
Warwickshire CV8 2LG   0203 56131

National Hedge Laying Society
NFYFC, National Agricultural Centre,
Kenilworth, Warwickshire CV8 2LG,
0203 56131

National Trust for Places of Historic Interest or
Natural Beauty
36 Queen Anne's Gate, London SW1H 9AS
01 222 9251

National Trust for Scotland
5 Charlotte Square, Edinburgh EH2 4DU
031 225 5922

Nature Conservancy Council
Northminster House, Peterborough
PE1 1UA   0733 40345

The Open Spaces Society
25a Bell Street, Henley on Thames, Oxon
RG9 2BA   0491 573535

The Ramblers' Association
1/5 Wandsworth Road, London SW8 2LJ
01 582 6826

Royal Society for Nature Conservation
The Green, Nettleham, Lincoln LN2 2NR
0522 752326

Royal Society for the Protection of Birds
The Lodge, Sandy, Bedfordshire SG19 2DL
0767 80551

Scottish Conservation Projects Trust
Head Office: Balallan House, 24 Allan Park,
Stirling FK8 2QG   0786 79697

Scottish Landowners' Federation
18 Abercromby Place, Edinburgh EH3 6TY
031 556 4466

Scottish Rights of Way Society
28 Rutland Square, Edinburgh EH1 2BW

Scottish Wildlife Trust
25 Johnston Terrace Edinburgh EH1 2NH
031 226 4602

Town and Country Planning Association
17 Carlton House Terrace, London SW1Y 5AS
01 930 8903

The Tree Council
Agriculture House, Knightsbridge, London
SW1X 7NJ   01 235 8854

Woodland Trust
Autumn Park, Dysart Road, Grantham,
Lincs NG31 6LL   0476 74297

World Wildlife Fund
Panda House, 11-13 Ockford Road, Godalming
Surrey GU7 1QU   048 68 20551

Bibliography

Books and major articles on hedging are listed below, along with works which place hedgerow management in the context of nature conservation and land use planning. Hedging, like other country crafts, is attracting increasing attention from the media, and more information is becoming available. Newspaper and magazine articles are often well illustrated with photographs and many are worth consulting for practical tips.

Museums, especially county museums in hedging areas, can be approached not only for displays but also for names and addresses of craftsmen with whom they may have had contact. Of particular importance is the work done by the Welsh Folk Museum, St Fagans, Cardiff. The hedges on the Museum grounds are managed according to various local traditions appropriate to the restored cottages and farm buildings which they surround. An indoor exhibit illustrates some of the major Welsh styles, including techniques and tools, based on the research of Mr Elfyn Scourfield, Assistant Curator.

Agricultural Training Board — Maintaining and constructing boundaries Leaflets LBM 2.B.1-7. Practical guides on the mechanical cutting of hedges and machine maintenance.

Agricultural Training Board — Hedge-laying Booklets LBM 2.B.8.TA 1 on 'Hedging tools'and LBM 2.B.8.TA 2 on 'Hedging.' Trainee chart LBM 2.B.8.TC. on 'Preparing hedge-laying tools'. All available from the ATB, 32-34 Beckenham Road, Beckenham, Kent BR3 4PB.

Beddall, J L (1950) — Hedges for Farm and Garden Faber & Faber Good coverage of suitable plants, planting and early care. Out of print, but possibly available through libraries.

Caborn J A (1965) — Shelterbreaks and Windbreaks Faber & Faber Trees for shelterbelts.

Countryside Commission — Countryside Conservation Handbook A series of leaflets, including Leaflet 2 (1979) 'Dutch Elm Disease - dealing with the aftermath', Leaflet 7 (1980) 'Hedge Management' and Leaflet 9 (1982) 'Tree Tagging'.

Countryside Commission (1974) — New Agricultural Landscapes Countryside Commission. A study of changing farm patterns in seven lowland areas, and a strategy for the maintenance of amenity and wildlife alongside agricultural productivity.

Countryside Commission (1984) — Agricultural Landscapes - A Second Look Countryside Commission. Report on the changes in the seven study areas of 'New Agricultural Landscapes'.

Countryside Commission (1984) — Agricultural Landscapes - Demonstration Farms Report of the Demonstration Farms Project 1975-82

Countryside Commission for Scotland — 'Shrubs for every site' Plant Information Sheet 1.3.2. CCS

Eaton, H J (1971) — 'Shelter Belts and Hedges' Agriculture May 1971 pp 185-9. A report of planting trials in exposed conditions in Cornwall.

Farming and Wildlife Advisory Group (1982) — Trees and Shrubs for Wildlife and the Landscape FWAG A guide to planting.

Farming and Wildlife Advisory Group (1983) — A Hedgerow Code of Practice FWAG

Hart, Edward (1981) — Hedge laying and fencing Thorsons

Hooper, M D and Holdgate, M W (eds) (1968) — Hedges and Hedgerow Trees Nature Conservancy Council Proceedings of Monks Wood Symposium No 4.

Hoskins, W G (1955) — The Making of the English Landscape Hodder and Stoughton. Penguin (1970)

Jackman, L (1976) — Exploring the Hedgerow Evans Brothers

James, N D G (1972) — The Arboriculturalist's Companion Blackwell Concise, practical chapters on hedges and hedgerow trees.

Jennings, Terry (1978) — World of a Hedge Faber & Faber

LeSueur, A D C (1951) — Hedges, Shelterbelts and Screens Country Life The basic source book along with that by Beddall, although both deal more with garden than with farm hedges.

Leigh Pemberton, J — Hedges Ladybird Good childrens book for hedgerow wildlife and plant identification.

Ministry of Agriculture, Fisheries and Food (1982) — Managing Farm Hedges Leaflet 762 MAFF Mechanical cutting, hedge laying.

Ministry of Agriculture, Fisheries and Food (1982) — Planting Farm Hedges Leaflet 763 MAFF Descriptions of species and methods of planting.

Nature Conservancy Council (1979) — Hedges and Shelterbelts NCC One in a series of conservation management leaflets.

Nature Conservancy Council (1981) — Nature Conservation and Agriculture - a series of projects for secondary schools. Project 3: Hedgerows and Walls Useful booklet with summary of conservation factors, with classroom and field exercises.

Pollard E, Hooper M D, and Moore N W (1974) — Hedges Collins New Naturalist. An excellent survey of the natural history of hedgerows and their conservation problems and opportunities.

Pollard, Robert S W (1975) — Trees and the Law Arboriculture Association Leaflet No 6 in a series of advisory publications. Practical and concise.

Rule, Ann Louise (1974) — Hedge Building in Mid and West Cornwall Institute of Folk Life Studies, Dept of English, University of Leeds. An unpublished dissertation on the design and technique of building stone hedges.

Salter, Beatrice (1978) — Beech Hedgerow Study Exmoor National Park Committee

Soltner, Dominique (1973) — L'Arbre et la Haie Collections Sciences et Techniques Agricole. Ste Gemmes-sur-Loire. Modern management, especially planting techniques and machine trimming. In French.

Standing Conference for Local History (1971) — Hedges and Local History National Council of Social Service. Articles on the uses and problems of hedgerow dating. No longer available from the NCSS, but should be obtainable from libraries.

Sturrock, F and Cathie, J (1980) — Farm Modernisation and the Countryside Univ. of Cambridge, Dept. of Land Economy. The impact of increasing farm size and hedge removal on arable farms.

Terrasson, F and Tendron, G (1975) — Evolution and Conservation of Hedgerow Landscape in Europe Council of Europe Reasons for and against hedge removal; physical effects on erosion etc. Extensive bibliography of European publications.

Tinker, Jon (1974) — 'The End of the English Landscape' New Scientist 64: 5 Dec 1974: 722-27 An evaluation of the Countryside Commission's report 'New Agricultural Landscapes'.

White, John T (1980) — Hedgerow Ash & Grant Beautifully illustrated story of a hedge from Saxon times to the present.

Glossary

Bank   A raised earthwork, usually acting as a barrier and often faced with turf or stone. (v) To build or repair a bank.

Batter   The slope of a bank, hedge or wall expressed as an angle or as a ratio of horizontal to vertical dimensions.

Beaver   The thin twigs of the pleachers on the far or field side of a Midlands type bullock hedge.

Binding   Flexible wooden rods or wire laced along the top of a hedge to hold the pleachers in place. Also known as edders, ethering, heathers, heathering or winders (Leicestershire).

Bowing   Pleachers which are bent out before being tucked between two stakes, in order to protect the cut stools of other pleachers (Wales).

Brash   Small twiggy or thorny branches, also known as brush.

Bullock fence   Any bank, fence, hedge or wall, usually 4'-4'6" (1220mm-1370mm), designed to contain cattle.

Butt   The larger, basal end of a tree or branch.

Byrdn   Brushy deadwood cuttings pushed in at the base of a hedge to protect the cut stools (Montgomeryshire).

Cag   Short ends of a trimmed branch left on a pleacher to help hold other pleachers in place (Radnorshire Crop and Pleach).

Chain   The traditional unit of hedge measurement, 22 yards (20m). Occasionally hedges are measured in rods, poles or perches, all of which equal 5½ yards (5m).

Comb   The top or crown of a bank (Devon).

Coppice   The practice of periodically cutting down trees nearly to ground level and allowing them to regenerate.

Course   A horizontal layer of turfs.

Crook   A deadwood stem with a sharply hooked top, pushed down through a laid hedge to hold the pleachers in place. Also known as a tie (Wales and the South West).

Crop   A stem cut off where it emerges from the laid hedge and left to act as a living stake. Also known as a cropper, pole or standard (Wales).

Cut and lay   The process of cutting part way through a standing tree and then bending and positioning (laying or layering) the stem to form a barrier. Also known as cut and pleach, pleach, plash or (South West) steep and lay or stoop and lay.

Deadwood   Any wood which is cut or broken off completely.

Ditch   A long narrow trench dug as a boundary, barrier or drain. In Ireland and parts of Wales, a bank or other raised barrier.

Double brush   The practice of bringing in pleachers from both sides of a hedge to a central line of stakes in order to create a wide, symmetrical sheep fence (Wales).

Double dig   The process of preparing a planting bed in two stages, first by removing the soil to a depth of one spit and then by forking the soil at the bottom of the trench to further break it up.

Face   The steep side of a bank or wall.

Far side   The side of the hedge normally without a ditch or steep bank face, also known as the field side.

Fence   A structure serving as an enclosure, barrier or boundary, loosely used to include hedges, banks, ditches or dykes.

Forest transplant   A tree seedling which has germinated in the forest and is transplanted to a nursery bed or the ultimate planting site.

Hedge   A line of closely planted shrubs or low-growing trees forming a fence or boundary, usually one or two rows wide.

Laying   See 'Cut and lay'.

Leaders   The tallest shoots of a plant where most vertical growth takes place.

Ley farming   The practice of using a field for arable and pasture in rotation.

Livewood   Any wood which is not cut or broken off completely from the supply of nutrients from the roots.

Near side   The side of the hedge, normally with a ditch or steep bank face, from which most hedging work is done.

Packing   Tamped earth fill supporting the turfs or the facing stones in a bank.

Pleacher A live stem cut and laid to form a stock barrier. Also known as a plasher, plesher, pletcher, plusher, sear or stolling.

Pollard The practice of cutting a tree's branches back to the main stem and allowing new ones to sprout.

Quick A thorn, usually hawthorn, plant or hedge. Also known as quickset.

Shard A gap in a hedge or bank.

Sheep fence Any bank, fence, hedge or wall, usually lower than a bullock fence, designed primarily to contain sheep.

Single brush The practice of bringing in pleachers mainly from one side of a line of stakes to create a relatively narrow, rather asymmetrical hedge (Wales).

Spit A rough unit of depth measurement used in digging, equal to the length of a spade blade.

Stake A deadwood pole or post driven into the hedge to hold the pleachers in place.

Standard tree A nursery tree raised for several years, usually twice transplanted and allowed to grow to a height of 5' (1.5m), before being set out in its final location.

Stem The living trunk of a shrub or tree.

Stool The stump or cut base of a shrub or tree from which grow new shoots. Also known as the rootstock.

Stub The projecting portion of stem which remains to be trimmed off the stool after a pleacher is cut and laid. Also known as a stob or ear.

Sucker A shoot springing from a root or underground part of a stem at some distance from the parent plant and eventually becoming a separate individual.

Thatching A fault in turf hedging, when the bottom of one course of turfs is allowed to project over the top of the course below (Devon). Also known as datching (north Devon).

Thorn General term for the hawthorn or whitethorn (Crataegus spp, usually C monogyna) or the blackthorn (Prunus spinosa).

Tiller A sapling, also known as a teller.

Top cut To trim the leaders of a shrub or tree at a point well above ground level.

Trim To cut back the smaller branches of a shrub or tree in order to keep the plant from growing too large or train it to a desired shape. Also known as breast, brush, pare or switch.

Turf Surface earth filled with the matted roots of grass etc, cut out for use in facing a bank; sod. (v) the process of cutting out and facing a bank with turfs.

White The freshly cut surface of a stool, pleacher or trimmed branch. Also known as burr (Wales).

This book is one of a series of handbooks on practical conservation work published by the British Trust for Conservation Volunteers.

Other titles in the series are Coastlands, Waterways and Wetlands, Dry Stone Walling, Woodlands, Footpaths and Fencing (Fencing being due for publication in September 1985).

The books are available in selected bookshops, or by mail order from the British Trust for Conservation Volunteers, 36 St Mary's Street, Wallingford, Oxfordshire OX10 0EU.